Cooking Light

BEST BAKING
RECIPES

Contact us

Web: CookingLight.com/contact-us
E-mail: CookingLight@customersvc.com

General correspondence
Mail: P.O. Box 1748
Birmingham, AL 35201
Phone: 800-336-0125

Back issues of special editions
Mail: P.O. Box 361095
Des Moines, IA 50336-1095
Phone: 800-633-4910

Subscriptions

Click the Subscribe link at
CookingLight.com, or call 800-336-0125.

CL annual cookbooks

To order our Cooking Light Annual Recipes
compilations, click CookingLight.com's
Books link, or call 800-633-4910.

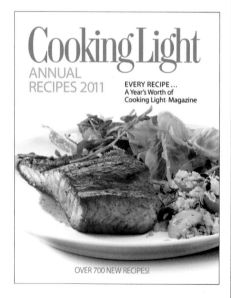

Cooking Light
ANNUAL
RECIPES 2011 — EVERY RECIPE...
A Year's Worth of
Cooking Light Magazine

OVER 700 NEW RECIPES!

Please Recycle This Magazine — Remove Inserts or Samples Before Recycling

Banana-Oatmeal
Chocolate Chip
Cookies, page 74

There's no sacrificing flavor or texture in our bakery goodies, but our portion sizes and nutrition profiles are smart and healthy.

I have to admit to a soft spot for homemade baked goods. From dinner rolls to pies to cookies, it's all good in my book. But the real reason I like to bake from scratch is that I like to know exactly what I'm eating. It's partly a quality control issue, but it's also about wanting to eat and enjoy breads, cakes, and cookies without feeling guilty about calories, fat, and sugar.

And I find that's no easy task when you buy from bakeries and restaurants. Just the other day I ordered a cupcake at a trendy bakery, and it was easily enough to serve at least two people. The icing was piled so high I felt a sugar coma coming on just looking at it.

In the *Cooking Light* world of bakery goodies, the flavors and ingredients I love are all there, but the portions and nutrition profiles are smart and healthy. Our recipe developers tweak and test a cupcake, brownie, or pie recipe until they find just the right amount of sugar and fat needed for flavor and texture without going overboard. What you'll find with our light style of baking is that technique is critical. Since fat levels are lower and sugar amounts often drop, it's important to weigh or measure flour carefully to produce light textures.

Keep that technique in mind when you check out some of our newest and tastiest treats that both the experienced and novice baker will love. There's a scrumptious Peanut Butter Banana Bread (page 16) that my friends go wild over. I'm also partial to Flaky Dinner Rolls (page 29) and a super-easy Carrot Cake (page 81) that is always a crowd-pleaser for birthdays and dinner parties.

Mary Creel,
Editor

CONTENTS

15

15

34

Novice bakers will love how easy this loaf is to shape.

New York claims this dessert classic.

57

62

89

Basic Banana
Bread, page 15

quick breads

These easy recipes for muffins, tea breads, scones, and pancakes deliver all your favorite flavors: chocolate, banana, blueberry, pumpkin, and lemon.

Serve with a hearty vegetable soup or meaty stew.

Pumpkin-Parmesan Scones ▲

Hands-on time: 20 min. Total time: 40 min.
Canned pumpkin puree makes these scones moist and tender, and it imbues them with the antioxidant beta-carotene. The small bits of flour-coated butter will melt during baking, yielding a tender, flaky scone.

6.75 ounces all-purpose flour (about 1½ cups)
2.375 ounces whole-wheat flour (about ½ cup)
2 teaspoons baking powder
½ teaspoon baking soda
½ teaspoon salt
¼ cup chilled butter, cut into small pieces
½ cup canned pumpkin
½ cup plain fat-free yogurt
2 large egg whites, divided
2 tablespoons grated fresh Parmesan cheese
1 tablespoon pumpkinseed kernels

1. Preheat oven to 400°.
2. Weigh or lightly spoon flours into dry measuring cups; level with a knife.

Combine flours, baking powder, baking soda, and salt in a large bowl; cut in butter with a pastry blender or 2 knives until mixture resembles coarse meal. Combine pumpkin, yogurt, and 1 egg white, stirring with a whisk. Add pumpkin mixture to flour mixture; stir just until moist.
3. Turn dough out onto a lightly floured surface; knead lightly 4 times with floured hands. Pat dough into an 8-inch circle on a baking sheet lined with parchment paper. Cut dough into 12 wedges, cutting into but not through dough. Brush remaining 1 egg white over top of dough. Sprinkle dough with cheese and pumpkinseeds, pressing lightly to adhere. Bake at 400° for 20 minutes or until golden. Slice scones along score lines with a serrated knife. Serve warm. Yield: 12 servings (serving size: 1 wedge).

CALORIES 129; **FAT** 4.9g (sat 2.7g, mono 1.2g, poly 0.5g); **PROTEIN** 4.4g; **CARB** 17.6g; **FIBER** 1.4g; **CHOL** 11mg; **IRON** 1.3mg; **SODIUM** 253mg; **CALC** 83mg

Whole-Wheat Buttermilk Pancakes ▶

Hands-on time: 15 min. Total time: 15 min.
Light, fluffy flapjacks, topped with butter and drizzled with syrup, guarantee you'll start the day off right. Top with fresh fruit, if you wish.

3.4 ounces all-purpose flour (about ¾ cup)
3.6 ounces whole-wheat flour (about ¾ cup)
3 tablespoons sugar
1½ teaspoons baking powder
½ teaspoon baking soda
½ teaspoon salt
1½ cups low-fat buttermilk
1 tablespoon canola oil
1 large egg
1 large egg white
Cooking spray
¾ cup maple syrup
3 tablespoons butter

1. Weigh or lightly spoon flours into dry measuring cups; level with a knife. Combine flours, sugar, and next 3 ingredients (through salt) in a large bowl, stirring with a whisk. Combine buttermilk, oil, egg, and egg white, stirring with a whisk. Add buttermilk mixture to flour mixture, stirring just until moist.
2. Heat a nonstick griddle or nonstick skillet over medium heat. Coat pan with cooking spray. Spoon about ¼ cup batter per pancake onto griddle. Turn pancakes over when tops are covered with bubbles and edges look cooked. Serve with syrup and butter. Yield: 6 servings (serving size: 2 pancakes, 2 tablespoons syrup, and 1½ teaspoons butter).

CALORIES 347; **FAT** 9.9g (sat 4.4g, mono 3.4g, poly 1.3g); **PROTEIN** 7.4g; **CARB** 59.2g; **FIBER** 2.3g; **CHOL** 53mg; **IRON** 2.1mg; **SODIUM** 520mg; **CALC** 197mg

{ fyi }

Pour the batter into the center of the hot griddle, and let it spread—don't pour in a circle. Once bubbles surface, slide a wide nylon spatula under the pancake. Quickly flip, and cook two more minutes.

Almond-Cranberry Corn Bread ◄

Hands-on time: 15 min. Total time: 35 min. Nut meals can replace up to one-fourth of the all-purpose flour in baked goods. Almond meal's hearty texture works well in corn bread. Look for it at health-food stores or from Bob's Red Mill (bobsredmill.com). Or place about 1 cup blanched almonds in a food processor, and process until finely ground. If you don't have a cast-iron skillet, you can also bake the bread at 400° in an 8-inch round cake pan for 16 minutes.

3 ounces all-purpose flour (about ²/₃ cup)
²/₃ cup yellow cornmeal
²/₃ cup almond meal
¹/₃ cup sugar
1 teaspoon baking powder
¹/₂ teaspoon baking soda
¹/₂ teaspoon salt
1¹/₂ tablespoons canola oil
1¹/₂ tablespoons sliced almonds
³/₄ cup nonfat buttermilk
¹/₂ cup dried cranberries
2 large egg whites
Cooking spray

1. Preheat oven to 400°.
2. Weigh or lightly spoon flour into a dry measuring cup; level with a knife. Combine flour and next 6 ingredients (through salt) in a large bowl.
3. Heat a small skillet over high heat. Add oil to pan; swirl to coat. Add almonds to pan; cook 2 minutes or until lightly toasted, stirring frequently. Strain oil through a fine sieve into flour mixture. Set aside 1 tablespoon almonds. Add remaining 1¹/₂ teaspoons almonds to flour mixture. Combine buttermilk, dried cranberries, and egg whites; add to flour mixture, stirring until well blended.
4. Spoon batter into an 8-inch cast-iron skillet coated with cooking spray. Sprinkle reserved 1 tablespoon toasted almonds over batter. Bake at 400° for 20 minutes or until a wooden pick inserted in center comes out clean. Cool in pan 10 minutes on a wire rack. Yield: 12 servings (serving size: 1 wedge).

CALORIES 149; FAT 5.4g (sat 0.4g, mono 3.3g, poly 1.4g); PROTEIN 4g; CARB 21.9g; FIBER 1.9g; CHOL 0mg; IRON 0.5mg; SODIUM 218mg; CALC 45mg

Spread the mounds of thick batter with a spatula.

Carrot Cake Pancakes ▲

Hands-on time: 25 min. Total time: 25 min. These cakey flapjacks feature warm spices and bright carrot flavor. Our lightened version calls for low-fat buttermilk and uses a small dab of honey butter to top the pancakes.

5.6 ounces all-purpose flour (about 1¹/₄ cups)
¹/₄ cup chopped walnuts, toasted
2 teaspoons baking powder
1 teaspoon ground cinnamon
¹/₄ teaspoon salt
¹/₈ teaspoon grated fresh nutmeg
Dash of ground cloves
Dash of ground ginger
¹/₄ cup brown sugar
³/₄ cup low-fat buttermilk
1 tablespoon canola oil
1¹/₂ teaspoons vanilla extract
2 large eggs, lightly beaten
2 cups finely grated carrot (about 1 pound)
Cooking spray
3 tablespoons butter, softened
2 tablespoons honey

1. Weigh or lightly spoon flour into dry measuring cups, and level with a knife. Combine flour and the next 7 ingredients (through ginger) in a large bowl, stirring with a whisk. Combine ¹/₄ cup brown sugar and next 4 ingredients (through eggs); add sugar mixture to flour mixture, stirring just until moist. Fold in 2 cups carrot.
2. Heat a large nonstick skillet over medium heat. Coat pan with cooking spray. Spoon 4 (¹/₄ cup) batter mounds onto pan, spreading with a spatula. Cook for 2 minutes or until tops are covered with bubbles and edges look cooked. Carefully turn pancakes over; cook 1 minute or until bottoms are lightly browned. Repeat procedure twice with remaining batter. Combine butter and honey in a small bowl; serve with pancakes. Yield: 6 servings (serving size: 2 pancakes and about 2 teaspoons honey butter).

CALORIES 315; FAT 13.3g (sat 4.8g, mono 4.4g, poly 3.3g); PROTEIN 7.8g; CARB 41.6g; FIBER 2.2g; CHOL 78mg; IRON 2.3mg; SODIUM 381mg; CALC 177mg

Mini chocolate chips melt nicely for the glaze.

Oatmeal Pancakes ▶

Hands-on time: 15 min. Total time: 15 min.

1.1 ounces all-purpose flour (¹/₄ cup)
1 cup quick-cooking oats
1 tablespoon sugar
¹/₂ teaspoon baking powder
¹/₂ teaspoon baking soda
¹/₄ teaspoon ground cinnamon
¹/₈ teaspoon salt
1 cup nonfat buttermilk
2 tablespoons butter, melted
1 large egg
Cooking spray

1. Weigh or lightly spoon flour into a dry measuring cup; level with a knife. Combine the first 7 ingredients in a medium bowl, stirring with a whisk.
2. Combine buttermilk, butter, and egg in a small bowl. Add to flour mixture, stirring just until moist.
3. Heat a nonstick griddle over medium heat. Coat pan with cooking spray. Spoon about 2¹/₂ tablespoons batter per pancake onto griddle. Turn pancakes over when tops are covered with bubbles; cook until bottoms are lightly browned. Yield: 3 servings (serving size: 4 pancakes).

CALORIES 273; **FAT** 11.2g (sat 5.7g, mono 3.3g, poly 1.3g); **PROTEIN** 10g; **CARB** 34.7g; **FIBER** 2.8g; **CHOL** 91mg; **IRON** 2.1mg; **SODIUM** 526mg; **CALC** 184mg

Banana-Chocolate-Walnut Bread ▲

Hands-on time: 15 min. Total time: 1 hr. 20 min.

1¹/₂ cups mashed ripe banana
¹/₃ cup plain fat-free yogurt
5 tablespoons butter, melted
2 large eggs
¹/₃ cup granulated sugar
¹/₃ cup packed light brown sugar
6.75 ounces all-purpose flour (about 1¹/₂ cups)
¹/₄ cup ground flaxseed
³/₄ teaspoon baking soda
¹/₂ teaspoon salt
¹/₂ teaspoon ground cinnamon
¹/₈ teaspoon ground allspice
²/₃ cup semisweet chocolate minichips, divided
¹/₃ cup chopped walnuts, toasted and divided
Cooking spray
2 tablespoons fat-free milk

1. Preheat oven to 350°.
2. Combine first 4 ingredients in a large bowl; beat with a mixer at medium speed until blended. Add sugars; beat until blended.
3. Weigh or lightly spoon flour into dry measuring cups; level with a knife. Combine flour and next 5 ingredients (through allspice) in a small bowl; stir well with a whisk. Add flour mixture to banana mixture; beat just until blended.
4. Fold ¹/₃ cup minichips and nuts into batter; pour batter into a 9 x 5–inch loaf pan coated with cooking spray. Bake at 350° for 55 minutes or until a wooden pick inserted in center comes out clean. Remove from oven; cool 10 minutes in pan on a wire rack. Remove bread from pan, and cool completely on wire rack. Combine remaining ¹/₃ cup minichips and milk in a microwave-safe bowl; microwave at HIGH for 30 seconds, stirring until smooth. Drizzle over bread. Yield: 16 servings (serving size: 1 slice).

CALORIES 195; **FAT** 8.9g (sat 4g, mono 2.3g, poly 2.1g); **PROTEIN** 3.6g; **CARB** 27.3g; **FIBER** 2.1g; **CHOL** 32mg; **IRON** 1.2mg; **SODIUM** 174mg; **CALC** 29mg

{ fyi }

Pancakes are easy even on busy weekdays. Mix the dry ingredients the night before. In the morning, whisk the wet ingredients together, and pour into the flour mixture; stir until smooth. Use the batter immediately or it will thicken. Sprinkle a few drops of water on the hot griddle; if the drops dance and evaporate in a few seconds, the pan is ready.

Fresh peach slices
and blueberries make a
colorful garnish.

French Toast with Maple-Apple Compote ◄

Hands-on time: 35 min. Total time: 35 min.

Compote:
Cooking spray
1 tablespoon butter
3 cups sliced peeled Pink Lady apples (about 1½ pounds)
¼ cup maple syrup
½ teaspoon ground cinnamon
French toast:
2 tablespoons granulated sugar
1 teaspoon ground cinnamon
1 cup 2% reduced-fat milk
2 teaspoons vanilla extract
⅛ teaspoon salt
4 large eggs, lightly beaten
12 (1-ounce) slices challah bread
4 teaspoons butter

1. Preheat oven to 250°. Place wire rack on a baking sheet, and place in oven.
2. To prepare compote, heat a large nonstick skillet over medium-high heat. Coat pan with cooking spray; melt 1 tablespoon butter in pan. Add apples to pan; sauté 8 minutes or until tender. Stir in maple syrup and ½ teaspoon cinnamon. Keep warm.
3. To prepare French toast, combine granulated sugar and 1 teaspoon cinnamon in a medium bowl, stirring with a whisk. Add milk, vanilla extract, salt, and eggs; whisk until well blended. Working with 1 bread slice at a time, place bread slice into the milk mixture, turning gently to coat both sides.
4. Heat a large nonstick skillet over medium-high heat. Melt 1 teaspoon butter in pan. Add 3 coated bread slices; cook 2 minutes on each side or until lightly browned. Place on rack in oven to keep warm. Repeat procedure 3 times with cooking spray, remaining 3 teaspoons butter, and remaining 9 coated bread slices. Serve French toast with compote. Yield: 6 servings (serving size: 2 pieces toast and about ⅓ cup compote).

CALORIES 370; **FAT** 12.1g (sat 5.3g, mono 4g, poly 1.3g); **PROTEIN** 11.3g; **CARB** 55.3g; **FIBER** 2.9g; **CHOL** 185mg; **IRON** 2.7mg; **SODIUM** 427mg; **CALC** 146mg

Chocolate Chip Scones ▲

Hands-on time: 10 min. Total time: 35 min.

½ cup currants, chopped
2 tablespoons water
3 cups low-fat baking mix (such as reduced-fat Bisquick)
5 tablespoons sugar, divided
½ teaspoon ground cinnamon
2 tablespoons butter, chilled and cut into small pieces
⅔ cup fat-free half-and-half
2 tablespoons semisweet chocolate minichips
1 large egg, separated
1 tablespoon fat-free half-and-half
½ cup powdered sugar
1½ teaspoons water

1. Preheat oven to 400°.
2. Combine ½ cup currants and 2 tablespoons water in a microwave-safe bowl. Microwave at HIGH for 45 seconds, stirring every 15 seconds. Cool 10 minutes (do not drain).
3. Combine baking mix, ¼ cup granulated sugar, and cinnamon in a large bowl. Cut in butter with 2 knives until mixture resembles coarse meal. Add currants, ⅔ cup half-and-half, chips, and egg white; stir until just moist. Drop dough by ¼ cupfuls onto a foil-lined baking sheet; place in freezer 5 minutes. Combine egg yolk and 1 tablespoon half-and-half; brush over tops, and sprinkle with the remaining granulated sugar. Bake at 400° for 12 minutes or until golden.

Cool on a wire rack.
4. Combine powdered sugar and 1½ teaspoons water; drizzle over scones. Yield: 1 dozen (serving size: 1 scone).

CALORIES 205; **FAT** 4.8g (sat 1.7g, mono 2g, poly 0.5g); **PROTEIN** 3.2g; **CARB** 37.9g; **FIBER** 1g; **CHOL** 23mg; **IRON** 1.4mg; **SODIUM** 360mg; **CALC** 133mg

Basic Banana Bread

Hands-on time: 15 min. Total time: 1 hr. 20 min. Look for whole ground flaxseed (sometimes labeled "flaxseed meal") on the baking aisle. This bread is shown on page 6.

1½ cups mashed ripe banana
⅓ cup plain fat-free yogurt
5 tablespoons butter, melted
2 large eggs
½ cup granulated sugar
½ cup packed brown sugar
6.75 ounces all-purpose flour (about 1½ cups)
¼ cup ground flaxseed
¾ teaspoon baking soda
½ teaspoon salt
½ teaspoon ground cinnamon
⅛ teaspoon ground allspice
Cooking spray
⅓ cup powdered sugar
1½ teaspoons 1% low-fat milk

1. Preheat oven to 350°.
2. Combine first 4 ingredients in a large bowl; beat with a mixer at medium speed. Add granulated and brown sugars; beat until combined.
3. Weigh or lightly spoon flour into dry measuring cups; level with a knife. Combine flour and next 5 ingredients (through ground allspice). Add flour mixture to banana mixture; beat just until blended. Pour batter into a 9 x 5–inch loaf pan coated with cooking spray. Bake at 350° for 55 minutes or until a wooden pick inserted in center comes out clean. Remove from oven; cool 10 minutes in pan on a wire rack. Remove bread from pan; cool completely. Combine powdered sugar and milk, stirring until smooth; drizzle over bread. Yield: 16 servings (serving size: 1 slice).

CALORIES 167; **FAT** 5.1g (sat 2.5g, mono 1.3g, poly 0.9g); **PROTEIN** 2.9g; **CARB** 28.3g; **FIBER** 1.5g; **CHOL** 32mg; **IRON** 1mg; **SODIUM** 173mg; **CALC** 24mg

Fig, Applesauce, and Almond Breakfast Loaf ▲

Hands-on time: 20 min. Total time: 1 hr. 45 min.
Serve this bread with a little cream cheese and jam, if you wish.

Streusel:
2¹/₂ tablespoons brown sugar
2 tablespoons all-purpose flour
1¹/₂ tablespoons coarsely chopped almonds
1 tablespoon chilled butter, cut into small pieces
¹/₈ teaspoon ground cinnamon

Bread:
1 cup dried figs
¹/₂ cup boiling water
Cooking spray
1 tablespoon all-purpose flour
2 large egg whites
1 large egg
³/₄ cup applesauce
¹/₃ cup plain fat-free yogurt
¹/₄ cup canola oil
¹/₂ teaspoon almond extract
³/₄ cup granulated sugar
6.75 ounces all-purpose flour (about 1¹/₂ cups)
2.5 ounces whole-wheat flour (about ¹/₂ cup)
¹/₃ cup chopped almonds, toasted
1 teaspoon baking powder
1 teaspoon ground cinnamon
¹/₂ teaspoon salt
¹/₂ teaspoon baking soda

1. Preheat oven to 350°.
2. To prepare streusel, combine first 5 ingredients in a small bowl, stirring with a fork until crumbly; set aside.
3. To prepare bread, combine figs and ¹/₂ cup boiling water in a small bowl; let stand 30 minutes. Coat 2 (8-inch) loaf pans with cooking spray; dust with 1 tablespoon flour.
4. Place egg whites and egg in a medium bowl; stir well with a whisk. Add applesauce, yogurt, oil, and almond extract; stir well. Add sugar, and stir well.
5. Weigh or lightly spoon 6.75 ounces all-purpose flour and 2.5 ounces whole-wheat flour into dry measuring cups; level with a knife. Combine flours and remaining ingredients in a large bowl, stirring with a whisk. Drain figs, and coarsely chop. Add figs and applesauce mixture to flour mixture, stirring until just combined. Divide batter between prepared pans. Sprinkle streusel over batter. Bake at 350° for 55 minutes or until a wooden pick inserted in center comes out clean. Cool in pans 15 minutes on a wire rack; remove from pans. Cool completely on wire rack. Yield: 2 loaves, 9 servings per loaf (serving size: 1 slice).

CALORIES 185; **FAT** 5.9g (sat 0.9g, mono 3.1g, poly 1.5g); **PROTEIN** 3.8g; **CARB** 30.9g; **FIBER** 2.5g; **CHOL** 14mg; **IRON** 1.2mg; **SODIUM** 140mg; **CALC** 58mg

Peanut Butter Banana Bread ▶

Hands-on time: 20 min. Total time: 1 hr. 35 min.
A small amount of chopped roasted peanuts offers delightfully surprising crunch.

Bread:
1¹/₂ cups mashed ripe banana
¹/₃ cup plain fat-free yogurt
¹/₃ cup creamy peanut butter
3 tablespoons butter, melted
2 large eggs
¹/₂ cup granulated sugar
¹/₂ cup packed brown sugar
6.75 ounces all-purpose flour (about 1¹/₂ cups)
¹/₄ cup ground flaxseed
³/₄ teaspoon baking soda
¹/₂ teaspoon salt
¹/₂ teaspoon ground cinnamon
¹/₈ teaspoon ground allspice
2 tablespoons chopped dry-roasted peanuts
Cooking spray

Glaze:
¹/₃ cup powdered sugar
1 tablespoon 1% low-fat milk
1 tablespoon creamy peanut butter

1. Preheat oven to 350°.
2. To prepare bread, combine first 5 ingredients in a large bowl, and beat with a mixer at medium speed. Add granulated and brown sugars, and beat until blended.
3. Weigh or lightly spoon flour into dry measuring cups; level with a knife. Combine flour and next 5 ingredients (through allspice) in a small bowl. Add flour mixture to banana mixture; beat just until blended. Stir in nuts. Pour batter into a 9 x 5–inch loaf pan coated with cooking spray. Bake at 350° for 1 hour and 5 minutes or until a wooden pick inserted in center comes out clean. Remove from oven; cool 10 minutes in pan on a wire rack. Remove bread from pan; cool.
4. To prepare glaze, combine powdered sugar, milk, and 1 tablespoon peanut butter in a small bowl, stirring with a whisk. Drizzle glaze over bread. Yield: 16 servings (serving size: 1 slice).

CALORIES 198; **FAT** 7.4g (sat 2.3g, mono 2.7g, poly 1.8g); **PROTEIN** 4.7g; **CARB** 29.7g; **FIBER** 1.9g; **CHOL** 28mg; **IRON** 1.1mg; **SODIUM** 200mg; **CALC** 27mg

Cognac or dark rum
adds depth of flavor to this
grown-up variation.

Bananas Foster Bread ◀

Hands-on time: 18 min. Total time: 1 hr. 28 min.
This adult interpretation switches all of the sugar to brown sugar and cooks the mashed bananas with butter and cognac or dark rum. And it's topped with a spiked glaze.

1¹/₂ cups mashed ripe banana
1 cup packed brown sugar, divided
6 tablespoons butter, melted and divided
¹/₄ cup cognac or dark rum, divided
¹/₃ cup plain fat-free yogurt
2 large eggs
6.75 ounces all-purpose flour (about 1¹/₂ cups)
¹/₄ cup ground flaxseed
³/₄ teaspoon baking soda
¹/₂ teaspoon salt
¹/₂ teaspoon ground cinnamon
¹/₈ teaspoon ground allspice
Cooking spray
¹/₃ cup powdered sugar

1. Preheat oven to 350°.
2. Combine banana, ¹/₂ cup brown sugar, 5 tablespoons butter, and 3 tablespoons cognac in a nonstick skillet. Cook over medium heat until mixture begins to bubble. Remove from heat; cool. Place banana mixture in a large bowl. Add yogurt, remaining ¹/₂ cup brown sugar, and eggs. Beat with a mixer at medium speed.
3. Weigh or lightly spoon flour into dry measuring cups; level with a knife. Combine flour and next 5 ingredients (through allspice) in a small bowl. Add flour mixture to banana mixture; beat just until blended. Pour batter into a 9 x 5–inch loaf pan coated with cooking spray. Bake at 350° for 1 hour or until a wooden pick inserted in center comes out clean. Remove from oven; cool 10 minutes in pan on a wire rack. Remove bread from pan; place on wire rack.
4. Combine remaining 1 tablespoon melted butter, remaining 1 tablespoon cognac, and the powdered sugar; stir until well blended. Drizzle over the warm bread. Yield: 16 servings (serving size: 1 slice).

CALORIES 194; FAT 5.8g (sat 3g, mono 1.5g, poly 0.9g); PROTEIN 2.9g; CARB 31.1g; FIBER 1.5g; CHOL 34mg; IRON 1.1mg; SODIUM 181mg; CALC 32mg

This loaf makes a nice hostess gift during the holidays.

Pecan-Topped Pumpkin Bread ▲

Hands-on time: 18 min. Total time: 1 hr. 18 min.
This recipe makes two loaves. Freeze the extra bread, tightly wrapped in plastic wrap, for up to one month. Check the bread after 50 minutes of baking—you may need to cover the loaves with aluminum foil for the last 10 minutes to prevent overbrowning. Omit the nuts or substitute chopped walnuts, if you prefer.

15 ounces all-purpose flour (about 3¹/₃ cups)
1 tablespoon baking powder
2 teaspoons baking soda
1 teaspoon salt
1 teaspoon ground cinnamon
1 teaspoon ground nutmeg
¹/₂ teaspoon ground allspice
2 cups sugar
¹/₂ cup egg substitute
¹/₂ cup canola oil
¹/₂ cup low-fat buttermilk
2 large eggs
²/₃ cup water
1 (15-ounce) can pumpkin
Cooking spray
¹/₃ cup chopped pecans

1. Preheat oven to 350°.
2. Weigh or lightly spoon flour into dry measuring cups; level with a knife. Combine flour and next 6 ingredients (through allspice) in a bowl, stirring with a whisk.
3. Place sugar, egg substitute, oil, buttermilk, and eggs in a large bowl; beat with a mixer at high speed until well blended. Add ²/₃ cup water and pumpkin, beating at low speed until blended. Add flour mixture to pumpkin mixture, beating at low speed just until combined. Spoon the batter into 2 (9 x 5–inch) loaf pans coated with cooking spray. Sprinkle pecans evenly over batter. Bake at 350° for 1 hour or until a wooden pick inserted in center comes out clean. Cool 10 minutes in pans on a wire rack; remove from pans. Cool completely on wire rack. Yield: 2 loaves, 12 servings per loaf (serving size: 1 slice).

CALORIES 198; FAT 6.6g (sat 0.7g, mono 3.6g, poly 1.9g); PROTEIN 3.4g; CARB 32.3g; FIBER 1.2g; CHOL 18mg; IRON 1.4mg; SODIUM 287mg; CALC 53mg

Bacon-Cheddar Corn Muffins ▼

Hands-on time: 15 min. Total time: 40 min.

4.5 ounces all-purpose flour (about 1 cup)
3/4 cup yellow cornmeal
1/2 cup (2 ounces) shredded sharp cheddar cheese
2 tablespoons sugar
1 teaspoon baking powder
1 teaspoon baking soda
3/4 teaspoon ground cumin
1/4 teaspoon salt
4 center-cut bacon slices, cooked, drained, and crumbled
1 jalapeño pepper, seeded and minced
1¼ cups low-fat buttermilk
1/4 cup canola oil
1 large egg, lightly beaten
Cooking spray

1. Preheat oven to 375°.
2. Weigh or lightly spoon flour into a dry measuring cup; level with a knife. Combine flour and next 7 ingredients (through salt) in a large bowl, stirring with a whisk. Stir in bacon and jalapeño; make a well in center of mixture. Combine buttermilk, oil, and egg in a bowl, stirring well with a whisk. Add buttermilk mixture to flour mixture, stirring just until moist.
3. Place 12 muffin-cup liners in muffin cups; coat with cooking spray. Divide batter evenly among muffin cups. Bake at 375° for 15 minutes or until a wooden pick inserted in center comes out clean. Cool 5 minutes in pan on a wire rack. Yield: 12 servings (serving size: 1 muffin).

CALORIES 160; FAT 7.9g (sat 2g, mono 3.3g, poly 1.6g); PROTEIN 4.8g; CARB 17.7g; FIBER 0.9g; CHOL 23mg; IRON 0.9mg; SODIUM 299mg; CALC 89mg

Spiced Persimmon and Pecan Muffins ▶

Hands-on time: 24 min. Total time: 50 min. Traditional spiced muffins suddenly seem stylish when made with seasonal persimmons. This bright reddish-orange fruit ripens in the fall to early winter and contains a good amount of vitamin A and some vitamin C.

3/4 cup chopped pecans, divided
5.6 ounces all-purpose flour (about 1¼ cups)
4.75 ounces whole-wheat flour (about 1 cup)
1/2 cup packed dark brown sugar
1½ teaspoons baking soda
1 teaspoon salt
1 teaspoon ground cinnamon
1/2 teaspoon ground nutmeg
1/8 teaspoon ground cloves
1 cup plain fat-free yogurt
1/3 cup ripe mashed Hachiya persimmon
1/3 cup honey
1/4 cup canola oil
2 teaspoons grated peeled fresh ginger
1 teaspoon vanilla extract
2 large eggs, lightly beaten
1/2 cup diced peeled Fuyu persimmon
1/2 cup dried cranberries
Cooking spray

1. Preheat oven to 375°.
2. Place ½ cup pecans in a single layer on a baking sheet. Bake at 375° for 8 minutes or until pecans are fragrant and toasted. Cool.
3. Weigh or lightly spoon flours into dry measuring cups, and level with a knife. Combine flours and next 6 ingredients (through cloves) in a bowl, stirring well with a whisk. Combine yogurt and next 6 ingredients (through eggs) in a bowl, stirring well with a whisk. Add egg mixture to flour mixture, and stir just until combined. Fold in Fuyu persimmon, cranberries, and toasted pecans. Spoon batter into 18 muffin cups coated with cooking spray. Sprinkle tops with remaining ¼ cup pecans.
4. Bake muffins at 375° for 18 minutes or until a wooden pick inserted in center comes out clean. Cool in pans for 5 minutes on a wire rack, and remove from pans. Yield: 18 servings (serving size: 1 muffin).

CALORIES 202; FAT 7.4g (sat 0.7g, mono 4.1g, poly 2.2g); PROTEIN 3.7g; CARB 31.8g; FIBER 2.4g; CHOL 20mg; IRON 1.2mg; SODIUM 255mg; CALC 36mg

Minced jalapeño and bacon speckle the batter.

{ fyi }

Both types of persimmons are used in this recipe. Creamy-fleshed Hachiya is mashed to keep the muffins moist. The firmer Fuyu variety is diced for fruity bits with some bite.

Blueberry Oatmeal Muffins ▶

Hands-on time: 15 min. Total time: 35 min. Tossing frozen blueberries with flour before adding them to the batter keeps them from turning the batter purple while they bake. Do not thaw the berries beforehand. If you use fresh blueberries, skip that step.

$1^2/_3$ cups quick-cooking oats
3 ounces all-purpose flour (about $^2/_3$ cup)
2.33 ounces whole-wheat flour (about $^1/_2$ cup)
$^3/_4$ cup packed light brown sugar
2 teaspoons ground cinnamon
1 teaspoon baking powder
1 teaspoon baking soda
$^3/_4$ teaspoon salt
$1^1/_2$ cups low-fat buttermilk
$^1/_4$ cup canola oil
2 teaspoons grated lemon rind
2 large eggs
2 cups frozen blueberries
2 tablespoons all-purpose flour
Cooking spray
2 tablespoons granulated sugar

1. Preheat oven to 400°.
2. Place oats in a food processor; pulse 5 to 6 times or until oats resemble coarse meal. Place in a large bowl.
3. Weigh or lightly spoon 3 ounces all-purpose flour (about $^2/_3$ cup) and whole-wheat flour into dry measuring cups; level with a knife. Add flours and next 5 ingredients (through salt) to oats; stir well with a whisk. Make a well in center of mixture.
4. Combine buttermilk and the next 3 ingredients (through eggs). Add to flour mixture; stir just until moist.
5. Toss blueberries with 2 tablespoons flour, and gently fold into batter. Spoon batter into 16 muffin cups coated with cooking spray, and sprinkle 2 tablespoons granulated sugar evenly over batter. Bake at 400° for 20 minutes or until muffins spring back when touched lightly in center. Remove from pans immediately; place on a wire rack. Yield: 16 servings (serving size: 1 muffin).

CALORIES 190; **FAT** 5g (sat 0.6g, mono 2.4g, poly 1.2g); **PROTEIN** 4.2g; **CARB** 33.3g; **FIBER** 2.4g; **CHOL** 23mg; **IRON** 1.6mg; **SODIUM** 248mg; **CALC** 74mg

Tuscan Lemon Muffins ▶

Hands-on time: 13 min. Total time: 29 min.

7.9 ounces all-purpose flour ($1^3/_4$ cups)
$^3/_4$ cup granulated sugar
$2^1/_2$ teaspoons baking powder
$^1/_4$ teaspoon salt
$^3/_4$ cup part-skim ricotta cheese
$^1/_2$ cup water
$^1/_4$ cup olive oil
1 tablespoon grated lemon rind
2 tablespoons fresh lemon juice
1 large egg, lightly beaten
Cooking spray
2 tablespoons turbinado sugar

1. Preheat oven to 375°.
2. Weigh or spoon flour into measuring cups; level with a knife. Combine flour and next 3 ingredients (through salt); make a well in center. Combine ricotta and next 5 ingredients (through egg). Add to flour mixture, stirring just until moist.
3. Place 12 muffin-cup liners in muffin cups; coat with cooking spray. Spoon batter into cups. Sprinkle turbinado sugar over batter. Bake at 375° for 16 minutes or until a pick inserted in center comes out clean. Cool 5 minutes in pan on a wire rack. Yield: 12 servings (serving size: 1 muffin).

CALORIES 186; **FAT** 6.2g (sat 1.5g, mono 3.4g, poly 0.6g); **PROTEIN** 4g; **CARB** 29.5g; **FIBER** 0.6g; **CHOL** 21mg; **IRON** 1mg; **SODIUM** 160mg; **CALC** 81mg

Chocolate–Chocolate Chip Muffins ▶

Hands-on time: 12 min. Total time: 27 min.

7.9 ounces all-purpose flour (about $1^3/_4$ cups)
$^1/_2$ cup packed brown sugar
$^1/_4$ cup unsweetened cocoa
1 teaspoon baking powder
1 teaspoon baking soda
$^1/_4$ teaspoon salt
1 cup warm water
$^1/_4$ cup canola oil
1 tablespoon red wine vinegar
1 teaspoon vanilla extract
1 large egg, lightly beaten
$^1/_2$ cup semisweet chocolate minichips, divided
Cooking spray

1. Preheat oven to 400°.
2. Weigh or lightly spoon flour into dry measuring cups; level with a knife. Combine flour and next 5 ingredients (through salt) in a large bowl, stirring with a whisk. Make a well in center of mixture. Combine 1 cup water and next 4 ingredients (through egg) in a bowl, stirring well with a whisk. Stir $^1/_4$ cup minichips into water mixture. Add water mixture to flour mixture, stirring just until moist.
3. Place 12 muffin-cup liners in muffin cups, and coat liners with cooking spray. Divide batter evenly among prepared muffin cups. Sprinkle remaining $^1/_4$ cup minichips evenly

over batter. Bake at 400° for 15 minutes or until a wooden pick inserted in center comes out clean. Cool for 5 minutes in pan on a wire rack. Yield: 12 servings (serving size: 1 muffin).

CALORIES 191; FAT 7.6g (sat 1.9g, mono 3.9g, poly 1.5g); PROTEIN 3.1g; CARB 29g; FIBER 1.5g; CHOL 15mg; IRON 1.5mg; SODIUM 197mg; CALC 37mg

Pistachio-Chai Muffins ▼

Hands-on time: 15 min. Total time: 30 min.

7.9 ounces all-purpose flour (about 1³⁄₄ cups)
¹⁄₂ cup packed brown sugar
1 teaspoon baking powder
1 teaspoon baking soda
¹⁄₄ teaspoon salt
2 chai blend tea bags
1 cup low-fat buttermilk

¹⁄₄ cup butter, melted
1¹⁄₂ teaspoons vanilla extract, divided
1 large egg, lightly beaten
Cooking spray
¹⁄₃ cup shelled dry-roasted pistachios, chopped
¹⁄₂ cup powdered sugar
1 tablespoon water

1. Preheat oven to 375°.
2. Weigh or lightly spoon flour into dry measuring cups; level with a knife. Combine flour and next 4 ingredients (through salt) in a large bowl, stirring with a whisk. Cut open tea bags; add tea to flour mixture, stirring well. Make a well in center of mixture. Combine buttermilk, butter, 1 teaspoon vanilla, and egg in a bowl, stirring well with a whisk. Add buttermilk mixture to flour mixture, stirring just until moist.
3. Place 12 muffin-cup liners in muffin cups; coat liners with cooking spray. Divide batter evenly among prepared muffin cups. Sprinkle nuts evenly over batter. Bake at 375° for 15 minutes or until a wooden pick inserted in center comes out clean. Cool for 5 minutes in pan on a wire rack.
4. Combine remaining ¹⁄₂ teaspoon vanilla, powdered sugar, and 1 tablespoon water, stirring until smooth. Drizzle evenly over muffins. Yield: 12 servings (serving size: 1 muffin).

CALORIES 192; FAT 6.2g (sat 2.8g, mono 2.1g, poly 0.8g); PROTEIN 3.9g; CARB 30.5g; FIBER 0.9g; CHOL 26mg; IRON 1.2mg; SODIUM 259mg; CALC 61mg

Lemon and olive oil are a classic Italian combo.

Sweet Challah,
page 30

yeast breads & rolls

Create light and lofty doughs that bake up perfect every time. From sweet cinnamon rolls to savory potato bread, it's all here.

Fresh Whole-Wheat Pitas ▶

Hands-on time: 25 min. Total time: 1 hr. 41 min. These are sublime straight out of the oven and stuffed with your favorite chicken or tuna salad or other sandwich fixings.

1 tablespoon sugar

1 package dry yeast (about 2¼ teaspoons)

1 cup plus 2 tablespoons warm water (100° to 110°)

10 ounces bread flour (about 2¼ cups)

4.75 ounces white whole-wheat flour (about 1 cup), divided (such as King Arthur or Bob's Red Mill)

2 tablespoons 2% reduced-fat Greek yogurt (such as Fage)

1 tablespoon extra-virgin olive oil

¾ teaspoon salt

Olive oil cooking spray

1. Dissolve sugar and yeast in 1 cup plus 2 tablespoons warm water in a large bowl; let stand 5 minutes. Weigh or lightly spoon flours into dry measuring cups; level with a knife. Add bread flour, 3 ounces (about ¾ cup) whole-wheat flour, yogurt, oil, and salt to the yeast mixture; beat with a mixer at medium speed until smooth. Turn the dough out onto a floured surface. Knead dough until smooth and elastic (about 10 minutes); add enough of remaining whole-wheat flour, 1 tablespoon at a time, to prevent dough from sticking to hands (dough will feel sticky). Place dough in a large bowl coated with cooking spray, turning to coat top. Cover and let rise in a warm place (85°), free from drafts, for 45 minutes or until doubled in size.

2. Position oven rack on the lowest shelf.

3. Preheat oven to 500°.

4. Divide dough into 8 portions. Working with one portion at a time, gently roll each portion into a 5½-inch circle. Place 4 dough circles on each of 2 baking sheets heavily coated with cooking spray. Bake, 1 sheet at a time, at 500° for 8 minutes or until puffed and browned. Cool on a wire rack. Yield: 8 servings (serving size: 1 pita).

CALORIES 211; FAT 2.9g (sat 0.4g, mono 1.5g, poly 0.4g); PROTEIN 7g; CARB 39.9g; FIBER 3.1g; CHOL 0mg; IRON 2.5mg; SODIUM 225mg; CALC 11mg

Whole-Wheat Cinnamon Rolls ▶

Hands-on time: 30 min. Total time: 2 hr. 25 min. Brown sugar sweetens the filling, and powdered sugar dissolves into a milky glaze that's drizzled over the top.

Dough:

1½ packages dry yeast (about 3¼ teaspoons)

¾ cup warm fat-free milk (100° to 110°)

¼ cup warm water (100° to 110°)

¼ cup butter, softened

¼ cup honey

½ teaspoon salt

1½ teaspoons fresh lemon juice

1 large egg

1 large egg white

11.25 ounces all-purpose flour, divided (about 2½ cups)

7 ounces whole-wheat flour (about 1½ cups)

Cooking spray

Filling:

¼ cup packed brown sugar

1½ tablespoons ground cinnamon

⅛ teaspoon ground nutmeg

⅓ cup raisins

Glaze:

¾ cup powdered sugar, sifted

¾ teaspoon vanilla extract

5 teaspoons fat-free milk

1. To prepare dough, dissolve yeast in warm milk and ¼ cup warm water in a large bowl; let stand 5 minutes or until foamy. Add butter and next 5 ingredients (through egg white); stir well. Weigh or lightly spoon flours into dry measuring cups; level with a knife. Add 9 ounces (about 2 cups) all-purpose flour and whole-wheat flour to yeast mixture, stirring until a soft dough forms. Turn dough out onto a floured surface. Knead until smooth and elastic (about 8 minutes); add enough of remaining ½ cup all-purpose flour, 1 tablespoon at a time, to prevent dough from sticking to hands (dough will feel sticky). Place dough in a large bowl coated with cooking spray, turning to coat top. Cover and let rise in a warm place (85°), free from drafts, 1 hour or until doubled in size. (Gently press two fingers into dough. If indentation remains, dough has risen enough.) Punch dough down; roll into a 16 x 12–inch rectangle on a floured surface. Coat surface of dough with cooking spray.

2. To prepare filling, combine brown sugar, cinnamon, and nutmeg; sprinkle over dough, leaving a ½-inch border. Sprinkle raisins over dough, pressing gently into dough. Roll up rectangle tightly, starting with a long edge, pressing firmly to eliminate air pockets; pinch seam to seal. Cut the dough into 16 rolls. Place the rolls, cut sides up, in a 13 x 9–inch baking pan coated with cooking spray. Cover and let rise 45 minutes or until doubled in size.

3. Preheat oven to 375°.

4. Uncover rolls. Bake at 375° for 22 minutes or until lightly browned. Cool in pan on a wire rack.

5. To prepare glaze, place powdered sugar and vanilla in a small bowl. Add 5 teaspoons milk, 1 teaspoon at a time, stirring to form a thick glaze. Drizzle glaze evenly over rolls. Yield: 16 servings (serving size: 1 roll).

CALORIES 209; FAT 3.7g (sat 2g, mono 0.9g, poly 0.3g); PROTEIN 5.1g; CARB 40.4g; FIBER 2.6g; CHOL 21mg; IRON 2mg; SODIUM 111mg; CALC 39mg

PREP TIP

If your dough rises too much, punch it back down and let it rise again. The texture might just be a little more dense.

BAKER'S SECRET
—
Sprinkle dough rectangle with sugar mixture and raisins; coat with cooking spray. Cover with plastic wrap; press to help toppings adhere.

Slices are good
toasted with a spot of
butter and jam.

Walnut Bread ◄

*Hands-on time: 40 min. Total time: 2 hr. 43 min.
This recipe calls for whole-wheat pastry flour,
a fine-textured, soft-wheat flour often used in
tender cakes and pastries. If unavailable, you
can substitute 1⅓ cups all-purpose flour and
⅔ cup cake flour.*

1¼ cups old-fashioned rolled oats
1 cup boiling water
**1 package dry yeast (about 2¼
    teaspoons)**
¼ cup warm water (100° to 110°)
1½ cups low-fat buttermilk
6 tablespoons honey
3 tablespoons canola oil
**20.25 ounces all-purpose flour
    (about 4½ cups), divided**
**9 ounces whole-wheat pastry flour
    (about 2 cups)**
2½ teaspoons salt
1 cup finely chopped walnuts
Cooking spray

1. Place oats in a food processor; pulse
8 times or until coarsely chopped.
Combine chopped oats and 1 cup
boiling water in a medium bowl; let
stand 10 minutes, stirring occasionally.
2. Dissolve yeast in ¼ cup warm water
in the bowl of a stand mixer; let stand
5 minutes. Add buttermilk to oat
mixture, stirring to combine. Stir in
honey and oil. Add the oat mixture to
yeast mixture; mix with dough hook
attachment until combined.
3. Weigh or lightly spoon 13.5 ounces
all-purpose flour (about 3 cups) and
whole-wheat pastry flour into dry
measuring cups; level with a knife.
Combine flours with salt. Add flour
mixture to buttermilk mixture. Mix
dough at medium speed 10 minutes
or until smooth and elastic, adding
remaining all-purpose flour, ¼ cup at a
time, to prevent dough from sticking
to sides of bowl. Add walnuts; mix at
medium speed just until combined.
4. Place dough in a large bowl coated
with cooking spray, turning to coat
top. Cover and let rise in a warm place
(85°), free from drafts, 1 hour or until
doubled in size. (Gently press two
fingers into dough. If indentation
remains, the dough has risen enough.)
5. Preheat oven to 400°.
6. Punch dough down; divide in half.

Divide each half into 3 equal portions.
Working with 1 portion at a time
(cover remaining dough to keep from
drying), shape each portion into a 14-
inch rope. Place 3 ropes lengthwise
on a baking sheet coated with cooking
spray (do not stretch). Pinch ends together at one end to seal. Braid ropes,
and pinch loose ends together to seal.
Repeat procedure with remaining
dough to form another braid. Cover
and let rise 30 minutes until doubled.
7. Spritz top and sides of loaves lightly
with water from a spray bottle. Bake
on center rack of oven at 400° for 28
minutes or until deep golden brown.
Remove from pan; cool on wire rack.
Yield: 2 loaves, 16 servings per loaf
(serving size: 1 slice).

CALORIES 150; **FAT** 4.3g (sat 0.5g, mono 1.2g, poly 2.2g);
PROTEIN 4.1g; **CARB** 24.1g; **FIBER** 2.1g; **CHOL** 1mg;
IRON 1.5mg; **SODIUM** 195mg; **CALC** 27mg

Flaky Dinner Rolls ▲

*Hands-on time: 45 min. Total time: 2 hr. 8 min.
Employing a simple folding technique twice
and allowing them to rise just once gives
these superlative rolls their flaky texture and
beautiful shape.*

3 tablespoons sugar
**1 package dry yeast (about 2¼
    teaspoons)**
**1 cup warm fat-free milk
    (100° to 110°)**
**13.5 ounces all-purpose flour
    (about 3 cups), divided**
¾ teaspoon salt
3 tablespoons butter, softened
Cooking spray

1. Dissolve sugar and yeast in warm
milk in a large bowl; let stand 5 minutes. Weigh or lightly spoon flour into
dry measuring cups; level with a knife.
Add 12.4 ounces (about 2¾ cups) flour
and salt to yeast mixture; stir until a
dough forms. Turn dough out onto a
lightly floured surface. Knead until
smooth (about 5 minutes); add enough
of remaining flour, 1 tablespoon at a
time, to prevent dough from sticking
to hands (dough will feel slightly
sticky). Cover dough with plastic
wrap, and let rest for 10 minutes.
2. Roll dough into a 12 x 10–inch
rectangle on a lightly floured baking
sheet. Gently spread butter over
dough. Working with a long side, fold
up bottom third of dough. Fold top
third of dough over the first fold to
form a 12 x 3–inch rectangle. Cover
with plastic wrap; place in freezer for
10 minutes.
3. Remove dough from freezer;
remove plastic wrap. Roll dough, still
on baking sheet (sprinkle on a little
more flour, if needed), into a 12 x 10–
inch rectangle. Working with a long
side, fold up bottom third of dough.
Fold top third of dough over the first
fold to form a 12 x 3–inch rectangle.
Cover with plastic wrap; place in
freezer for 10 minutes.
4. Remove dough from freezer;
remove plastic wrap. Roll dough, still
on baking sheet, into a 12 x 8–inch
rectangle. Beginning with a long side,
roll up dough, jelly-roll fashion; pinch
seam to seal (do not seal ends of roll).
Cut roll into 12 equal slices. Place
slices, cut sides up, in muffin cups
coated with cooking spray. Lightly
coat tops of dough slices with cooking
spray. Cover and let rise in a warm
place (85°), free from drafts, 45
minutes or until doubled in size.
5. Preheat oven to 375°.
6. Bake dough at 375° for 20 minutes
or until golden brown. Remove from
pan, and cool for 5 minutes on a wire
rack. Serve rolls warm. Yield: 12
servings (serving size: 1 roll).

CALORIES 160; **FAT** 3.2g (sat 1.5g, mono 1.2g, poly 0.2g);
PROTEIN 4.2g; **CARB** 28.3g; **FIBER** 1g; **CHOL** 8mg;
IRON 1.7mg; **SODIUM** 178mg; **CALC** 25mg

Monday Morning Potato Rolls and Bread ▶

Hands-on time: 45 min. Total time: 2 hr. 50 min.

1 cup mashed cooked peeled baking potatoes (about 8 ounces)
1 cup fat-free milk
3 tablespoons honey
2 tablespoons butter
21.4 ounces bread flour (about 4½ cups), divided
2½ teaspoons dry yeast
1½ teaspoons sea salt
2 large eggs
1 teaspoon olive oil
Cooking spray

1. Combine first 4 ingredients in a microwave-safe bowl. Microwave at HIGH for 2 minutes or until mixture is 110°. Stir with a whisk until smooth.
2. Weigh or lightly spoon flour into dry measuring cups; level with a knife. Combine 6.75 ounces (about 1½ cups) flour, yeast, and salt in a large mixing bowl. Add potato mixture to flour mixture, stirring with a fork until combined. Add eggs; stir until combined.
3. Add 9 ounces (about 2 cups) flour to potato mixture; stir until a soft dough forms. Turn dough out onto a floured surface. Knead until smooth and elastic (about 10 minutes); add enough of remaining 1 cup flour, 1 tablespoon at a time, to prevent dough from sticking to hands (dough will feel sticky).
4. Place dough in a large bowl coated with olive oil, turning to coat top. Cover and let rise in a warm place (85°), free from drafts, 1 hour or until doubled in size. (Gently press two fingers into dough. If indentation remains, dough has risen enough.) Punch dough down; cover and let rest 5 minutes.
5. Divide dough in half. Working with one portion at a time (cover remaining dough to prevent drying), roll one portion into a 14 x 7–inch rectangle on a floured surface. Roll up rectangle tightly, starting with a short edge, pressing firmly to eliminate air pockets; pinch seam and ends to seal. Place loaf, seam side down, in an 8 x 4–inch loaf pan coated with cooking spray.
6. Divide remaining portion into 9 portions, and shape each into a ball.

{ fyi }

Mashed potatoes give a basic white bread a softer texture, help it stay moist, and help it keep longer. They also lend great toasting qualities.

Place balls in an 8-inch square baking dish coated with cooking spray. Coat top of loaf and rolls with cooking spray. Cover and let rise in a warm place (85°), free from drafts, 30 minutes or until doubled in size. (Gently press two fingers into dough. If the indentation remains, dough has risen enough.)
7. Preheat oven to 350°.
8. Bake at 350° for 30 minutes or until tops of rolls are browned and loaf sounds hollow when tapped. Remove from pans; cool on wire racks. Yield: 18 servings (serving size: 1 roll or one-ninth of loaf).

CALORIES 168; **FAT** 2.8g (sat 1.1g, mono 0.8g, poly 0.4g); **PROTEIN** 5.7g; **CARB** 30.1g; **FIBER** 1.1g; **CHOL** 28mg; **IRON** 1.8mg; **SODIUM** 207mg; **CALC** 24mg

Sweet Challah

Hands-on time: 40 min. Total time: 3 hr. 28 min. Allowing the dough to rise three times gives the yeast more time to develop, resulting in a rich, complex flavor. Although this bread, shown on page 24, is best eaten the day it's made, you can also bake it a day in advance. Cool completely, wrap in plastic wrap, and then wrap in foil; store at room temperature. Leftovers make excellent bread pudding.

1 package dry yeast (about 2¼ teaspoons)
1 cup warm water (100° to 110°)
3 tablespoons honey
Dash of saffron threads, crushed
3 tablespoons butter, melted and cooled
1 teaspoon salt
1 large egg
14.25 ounces bread flour (about 3 cups), divided
Cooking spray
1 teaspoon cornmeal
1 teaspoon water
1 large egg yolk, lightly beaten
¼ teaspoon poppy seeds

1. Dissolve yeast in 1 cup warm water in a large bowl; stir in honey and saffron threads. Let stand for 5 minutes. Add melted butter, salt, and egg; stir well with a whisk.
2. Weigh or lightly spoon flour into dry measuring cups; level with a knife. Add 13 ounces (about 2¾ cups) flour to yeast mixture, and stir until a soft dough forms. Cover and let stand for 15 minutes.
3. Turn dough out onto a lightly floured surface. Knead until smooth and elastic (about 8 minutes); add enough of remaining flour, 1 tablespoon at a time, to prevent dough from sticking to hands (dough will be very soft).
4. Place dough in a large bowl coated with cooking spray, turning to coat top. Cover and let rise in a warm place (85°), free from drafts, 40 minutes or until doubled in size. (Gently press two fingers into dough. If indentation remains, the dough has risen enough.)
5. Punch dough down. Shape dough into a ball; return to bowl. Cover and let rise an additional 40 minutes or until doubled in size. Punch dough down; cover and let rest 15 minutes.
6. Divide dough into 3 equal portions. Working with 1 portion at a time (cover remaining dough to prevent drying), on a lightly floured surface, roll each portion into a 25-inch rope with slightly tapered ends. Place ropes lengthwise on a large baking sheet sprinkled with cornmeal; pinch the untapered ends together to seal. Braid ropes; pinch loose ends to seal. Cover and let rise 20 minutes or until almost doubled in size.
7. Preheat oven to 375°.
8. Combine 1 teaspoon water and egg yolk, stirring with a fork until blended. Uncover loaf, and gently brush with egg yolk mixture. Sprinkle evenly with poppy seeds. Bake at 375° for 30 minutes or until loaf sounds hollow when tapped. Cool on a wire rack. Yield: 1 loaf, 12 servings (serving size: 1 slice).

CALORIES 157; **FAT** 4.1g (sat 2.1g, mono 1.2g, poly 0.4g); **PROTEIN** 5g; **CARB** 26.9g; **FIBER** 0.9g; **CHOL** 42mg; **IRON** 1.7mg; **SODIUM** 222mg; **CALC** 7mg

The dough is more like a
thick batter. Too much flour
will result in dry rolls.

Cheese and Chive Challah ▶

Hands-on time: 40 min. Total time: 2 hr. 22 min.
The traditional yeasted egg bread is enriched
even more by adding cheese to the dough.
We love the flavor of fontina, but Gruyère or
another Swiss cheese would also work.

1 cup warm 2% reduced-fat milk
(100° to 110°)
1 teaspoon sugar
1 package dry yeast (about 2¼
teaspoons)
3 tablespoons butter, melted
1½ teaspoons salt
5 large egg yolks
3 large eggs
¾ cup (3 ounces) shredded aged
fontina cheese
½ cup finely chopped fresh chives
10.7 ounces bread flour (about 2¼
cups)
13.5 ounces all-purpose flour, divided
(about 3 cups)
Cooking spray
1 large egg
2 tablespoons water
2 tablespoons grated fresh
Parmigiano-Reggiano cheese

1. Combine first 3 ingredients in a
large bowl; let stand 5 minutes or until
bubbly. Stir in butter, salt, 5 egg yolks,
and 3 eggs. Stir in fontina and chives.
Weigh or lightly spoon flours into dry
measuring cups; level with a knife.
Add 10.7 ounces bread flour (about 2¼
cups) and 12.4 ounces (about 2¾ cups)
all-purpose flour to yeast mixture,
stirring until a soft dough forms
(dough will be sticky).
2. Turn dough out onto a lightly
floured surface. Knead until smooth
and elastic, adding remaining ¼ cup
all-purpose flour, 1 tablespoon at a
time, to prevent dough from sticking
to hands. Place dough in a large bowl
coated with cooking spray, turning to
coat top. Cover with plastic wrap, and
let rise in a warm place (85°), free
from drafts, for 45 minutes or until
doubled in size. Punch dough down;
cover and let rise 50 minutes or until
doubled in size. (Gently press two
fingers into dough. If indentation
remains, dough has risen enough.)
3. Divide dough into 6 equal portions.
Roll each portion into a ball. Roll each

ball into a rope about 15 inches long.
Place 3 ropes parallel to one another;
braid ropes. Pinch ends together, and
tuck under loaf. Repeat procedure with
remaining 3 ropes. Place loaves on a
baking sheet lined with parchment
paper; coat with cooking spray. Cover
and let rise 30 minutes or until doubled
in size.
4. Preheat oven to 375°.
5. Combine 1 egg and 2 tablespoons
water, stirring well with a whisk. Brush
loaves gently with egg mixture. Sprinkle loaves evenly with Parmigiano-
Reggiano. Bake at 375° for 25 minutes
or until golden. Remove from baking
sheet; cool on a wire rack. Yield: 24
servings (serving size: 1 slice).

CALORIES 160; FAT 4.7g (sat 2.3g, mono 1.5g, poly 0.5g);
PROTEIN 6.2g; CARB 22.5g; FIBER 0.8g; CHOL 78mg;
IRON 1.6mg; SODIUM 210mg; CALC 51mg

No-Knead Overnight Parmesan and Thyme Rolls ◀

Hands-on time: 25 min. Total time: 8 hr. 37 min.

½ teaspoon dry yeast
2 tablespoons warm water
(100° to 110°)
2 tablespoons extra-virgin olive oil,
divided
1 teaspoon dried thyme
⅓ cup 2% reduced-fat milk
½ cup (2 ounces) grated Parmigiano-
Reggiano cheese, divided
1 tablespoon sugar
½ teaspoon kosher salt
1 large egg, lightly beaten

1.1 ounces white whole-wheat white
flour (about ¼ cup)
5.6 ounces all-purpose flour
(about 1¼ cups), divided
Cooking spray
½ teaspoon cracked black
pepper

1. Dissolve yeast in 2 tablespoons
warm water in a large bowl; let stand
5 minutes or until bubbly.
2. Heat 1 tablespoon oil in a small
saucepan over medium heat. Add
thyme to pan; cook 1 minute or until
bubbly and fragrant. Add thyme
mixture and milk to yeast mixture,
stirring with a whisk; add ¼ cup cheese,
sugar, salt, and egg, stirring well.
3. Weigh or lightly spoon flours into
dry measuring cups; level with a knife.
Using a wooden spoon, stir whole-
wheat white flour into yeast mixture.
Add 1 cup all-purpose flour to yeast
mixture, stirring well. Add enough of
remaining ¼ cup all-purpose flour, 1
tablespoon at a time, to form a smooth
but very sticky dough. Place dough in
a large bowl coated with cooking
spray, turning to coat top. Cover and
refrigerate overnight. (Dough will not
double in size.)
4. Remove dough from refrigerator.
Do not punch dough down. Turn
dough out onto a floured surface;
sprinkle dough lightly with flour. Roll
dough into a 12 x 7–inch rectangle.
Brush dough with remaining 1 tablespoon oil. Sprinkle remaining ¼ cup
cheese and pepper evenly over dough.
Beginning with a long side, roll up
dough, jelly-roll fashion. Pinch seam
to seal (do not seal ends of roll). Cut
roll into 8 (1½-inch) slices. Place
slices, cut sides up, on a baking sheet
lined with parchment paper. Cover
and let rise in a warm place (85°), free
from drafts, 1 hour or until rolls have
risen slightly.
5. Preheat oven to 400°.
6. Place pan in oven, and immediately
reduce heat to 375°. Bake at 375° for
12 minutes or until golden brown.
Yield: 8 servings (serving size: 1 roll).

CALORIES 161; FAT 6.3g (sat 2g, mono 3.3g, poly 0.6g);
PROTEIN 6.3g; CARB 19.7g; FIBER 1.3g; CHOL 32mg;
IRON 1.4mg; SODIUM 246mg; CALC 112mg

Flour your hands to make dough handling easier.

Orange-Buttermilk Dinner Rolls ▲

Hands-on time: 25 min. Total time: 2 hr. 50 min.

**1¼ cups warm buttermilk
   (100° to 110°)**
2 tablespoons sugar
1 tablespoon honey
1 package dry yeast
**3 tablespoons butter, melted and
   divided**
4 teaspoons grated orange rind
1 teaspoon kosher salt
**14 ounces all-purpose flour
   (about 3 cups)**
Cooking spray

1. Combine first 3 ingredients in bowl of an electric mixer. Sprinkle yeast over milk mixture; let stand 5 minutes or until bubbly. Stir in 2 tablespoons butter, rind, and salt. Weigh or lightly spoon flour into dry measuring cups; level with a knife. Add flour to yeast mixture; mix on low speed with a dough hook until a soft, elastic dough forms (about 5 minutes). Dough will be sticky. Place dough in a large bowl coated with cooking spray, turning to coat top. Cover and let rise in a warm place (85°) for 1 hour or until doubled in size.
2. Punch dough down; turn out onto a lightly floured surface. Cut dough into 13 equal pieces. Working with 1 piece of dough at a time, roll dough into a ball by cupping your hand and push-ing against dough and surface while rolling. Arrange dough balls 2 inches apart on a baking sheet coated with cooking spray. Brush lightly with remaining 1 tablespoon butter. Cover; let rise 1 hour or until doubled in size.
3. Preheat oven to 375°.
4. Bake at 375° for 20 minutes or until rolls are golden. Remove rolls from pan; cool slightly on a wire rack. Yield: 13 rolls (serving size: 1 roll).

CALORIES 163; FAT 3.7g (sat 2.2g, mono 0.7g, poly 0.2g); PROTEIN 4.2g; CARB 28.1g; FIBER 1g; CHOL 10mg; IRON 1.5mg; SODIUM 192mg; CALC 7mg

Christmas Stollen ▶

*Hands-on time: 40 min. Total time: 2 hr. 32 min.
Order candied citron from amazon.com, or omit it and add extra dried apricots and increase the lemon rind to 1 tablespoon.*

**16.9 ounces all-purpose flour
   (about 3¾ cups), divided**
½ teaspoon salt
½ teaspoon freshly grated nutmeg
¼ cup fresh orange juice
2 tablespoons brandy
½ cup dried cherries
⅓ cup golden raisins
⅓ cup chopped dried apricots
**½ cup warm 2% reduced-fat milk
   (100° to 110°)**
¼ cup granulated sugar
1 package dry yeast
6 tablespoons butter, melted
2 large eggs, lightly beaten
½ cup diced candied citron
½ cup sliced almonds, toasted
1½ teaspoons grated lemon rind
Cooking spray
**2 tablespoons 2% reduced-fat milk,
   divided**
1 large egg
½ cup powdered sugar

1. Weigh or lightly spoon flour into dry measuring cups, and level with a knife. Combine 15.75 ounces (about 3½ cups) flour, salt, and nutmeg. Combine orange juice and brandy; microwave at HIGH 45 seconds. Add cherries, raisins, and apricots; let stand for 20 minutes.
2. Combine warm milk, granulated sugar, and yeast; let stand for 5 minutes. Stir butter and 2 eggs into yeast mixture. Stir in juice mixture, ½ cup citron, almonds, and rind. Add flour mixture to yeast mixture, stirring until a soft dough forms. Turn dough out onto a lightly floured surface. Knead 5 minutes or until dough is smooth and elastic, adding remaining ¼ cup flour, 1 tablespoon at a time, to prevent dough from sticking to hands (dough will feel sticky).
3. Place dough in a large bowl coated with cooking spray, turning to coat top. Cover and let rise in a warm place (85°) 1 hour or until doubled in size. Punch dough down. Divide dough into 2 equal portions; roll each into an 11 x 8–inch oval. Fold 1 short end toward center; fold other short end toward center until it overlaps first end. Place loaves, seam side down, on a baking sheet lined with parchment paper. Cover and let rise 1 hour or until doubled in size.
4. Preheat oven to 350°.
5. Combine 1 tablespoon milk and 1 egg. Uncover dough; brush gently with milk mixture. Bake at 350° for 32 minutes or until golden. Cool on wire racks. Combine 1 tablespoon milk and powdered sugar, stirring until smooth; drizzle over loaves. Yield: 24 servings (serving size: 1 slice).

CALORIES 168; FAT 4.8g (sat 2.2g, mono 1.7g, poly 0.5g); PROTEIN 3.8g; CARB 26.5g; FIBER 1.4g; CHOL 34mg; IRON 1.4mg; SODIUM 83mg; CALC 26mg

Wrap this fruited
bread in a tea towel
and tie with a pretty
ribbon for a lovely
homemade gift.

Chocolate Babka ◄

Hands-on time: 35 min. Total time: 3 hr. 40 min.
Sweet dough envelops a chocolaty filling in a bread you'll swoon over.

Dough:
1 teaspoon granulated sugar
1 package dry yeast (about 2¼ teaspoons)
¾ cup warm 1% low-fat milk (100° to 110°)
6 tablespoons granulated sugar
½ teaspoon vanilla extract
¼ teaspoon salt
1 large egg yolk, lightly beaten
7.5 ounces all-purpose flour (about 1⅔ cups), divided
5.85 ounces bread flour (about 1¼ cups)
5 tablespoons butter, cut into pieces and softened
Cooking spray
Filling:
½ cup granulated sugar
3 tablespoons unsweetened cocoa
½ teaspoon ground cinnamon
¼ teaspoon salt
4 ounces semisweet chocolate, finely chopped
Streusel:
2 tablespoons powdered sugar
1 tablespoon all-purpose flour
1 tablespoon butter, softened

1. Dissolve 1 teaspoon granulated sugar and yeast in warm milk in the bowl of a stand mixer; let stand 5 minutes. Stir in 6 tablespoons granulated sugar, vanilla extract, ¼ teaspoon salt, and egg yolk. Weigh or lightly spoon flours into dry measuring cups; level with a knife. Add 6 ounces (about 1⅓ cups) all-purpose flour and bread flour to milk mixture; beat with dough hook attachment at medium speed until well blended (about 2 minutes). Add 5 tablespoons butter, beating until well blended. Scrape dough out onto a floured surface (dough will be very sticky). Knead until smooth and elastic (about 10 minutes); add 1.5 ounces (about ⅓ cup) all-purpose flour, 1 tablespoon at a time, to prevent dough from sticking to hands (dough will be very soft).

2. Place dough in a large bowl coated with cooking spray, turning to coat top. Cover and let rise in a warm place

---

{ fyi }

To get a jump start on baking the Chocolate Babka, roll out dough, fill, shape, and refrigerate overnight in the pan. It will rise to the top of the pan in the refrigerator. In the morning, let it come to room temperature, top with streusel, and bake as directed.

(85°), free from drafts, 1½ hours or until doubled in size. (Gently press two fingers into dough. If indentation remains, dough has risen enough.) Punch dough down; cover and let dough rest 5 minutes.

3. Line the bottom of a 9 x 5–inch loaf pan with parchment paper; coat sides of pan with cooking spray.

4. To prepare filling, combine ½ cup granulated sugar, cocoa, cinnamon, salt, and chocolate in a medium bowl; set aside.

5. Place the dough on a generously floured surface; roll dough out into a 16-inch square. Sprinkle filling over dough, leaving a ¼-inch border around edges. Roll up dough tightly, jelly-roll fashion; pinch seam and ends to seal. Holding dough by ends, twist dough 4 times as if wringing out a towel. Fit dough into prepared pan. Cover and let rise 45 minutes or until doubled in size.

6. Preheat oven to 350°.

7. To prepare streusel, combine powdered sugar, 1 tablespoon all-purpose flour, and 1 tablespoon softened butter, stirring with a fork until mixture is crumbly; sprinkle streusel evenly over dough. Bake at 350° for 40 minutes or until loaf is browned on bottom and sounds hollow when tapped. Cool bread in pan 10 minutes on a wire rack; remove from pan. Cool bread completely on wire rack before slicing. Yield: 16 servings (serving size: 1 slice).

CALORIES 220; FAT 7.1g (sat 4.3g, mono 2g, poly 0.5g); PROTEIN 4.1g; CARB 36g; FIBER 1.5g; CHOL 25mg; IRON 1.4mg; SODIUM 111mg; CALC 23mg

---

Brioche Rolls ►

Hands-on time: 40 min. Total time: 12 hr. 14 min.
You don't need a brioche pan for this recipe—a muffin tin works well. Start a day ahead, as the overnight rise is essential for bakery-like flavor.

1 package dry yeast (about 2¼ teaspoons)
⅓ cup warm 1% low-fat milk (100° to 110°)
15.75 ounces all-purpose flour (about 3½ cups)
⅓ cup sugar
½ teaspoon salt
4 large eggs, lightly beaten
8½ tablespoons unsalted butter, softened and divided
Cooking spray
1 tablespoon water
1 large egg white

1. Dissolve yeast in warm milk in the bowl of a stand mixer fitted with the paddle attachment; let stand 5 minutes. Weigh or lightly spoon flour into dry measuring cups; level with a knife. Add flour, sugar, salt, and eggs to milk mixture; beat with mixer at low speed until smooth, scraping down sides of bowl with spatula as needed. Remove paddle attachment; insert dough hook. Mix dough at low speed 5 minutes or until soft and elastic and dough just begins to pull away from sides of bowl. Cut 6½ tablespoons butter into large cubes; add half of butter cubes to dough, mixing at medium speed to blend. Add remaining half of cubes to dough; mix at medium speed until incorporated. Mix dough on medium speed 4 minutes or until smooth and elastic. Place dough in a large bowl coated with cooking spray, turning to coat top. Cover and let rise in a warm place (85°), free from drafts, 1 hour or until doubled in size. (Gently press two fingers into dough. If indentation remains, dough has risen enough.) Punch dough down; form into a ball. Return dough to bowl; cover with plastic wrap, and refrigerate 8 hours or overnight.

2. Uncover dough; let stand 90 minutes or until dough is at room temperature. Divide dough into 4 equal portions. Working with one portion at a time (cover the remaining dough to prevent

drying), cut each portion into 6 equal pieces. Roll each piece into a 1½-inch ball. Repeat procedure with remaining 3 dough portions to make 24 rolls total. Place the rolls in muffin cups coated with cooking spray. Cover and let rise for 45 minutes or until almost doubled in size.

3. Preheat oven to 350°.

4. Combine 1 tablespoon water and egg white; stir with a whisk. Gently brush rolls with egg mixture. Bake at 350° for 14 minutes or until golden. Place pans on wire racks. Place remaining 2 tablespoons butter in a microwave-safe bowl; microwave at HIGH 20 seconds or until butter melts. Brush butter onto rolls. Yield: 24 rolls (serving size: 1 roll).

CALORIES 128; FAT 4.9g (sat 2.8g, mono 1.4g, poly 0.4g); PROTEIN 3.4g; CARB 17.2g; FIBER 0.6g; CHOL 41mg; IRON 1.1mg; SODIUM 94mg; CALC 13mg

Honey-Almond Focaccia with Rosemary ▶

Hands-on time: 35 min. Total time: 1 hr. 49 min.

½ cup sliced almonds
½ cup olive oil
1 tablespoon chopped fresh rosemary
⅛ teaspoon salt
⅛ teaspoon crushed red pepper
1 cup warm 1% low-fat milk (100° to 110°)
1½ teaspoons granulated sugar
1 package dry yeast
14.7 ounces all-purpose flour (about 3¼ cups), divided
1 teaspoon salt
1 large egg yolk
2 tablespoons olive oil, divided
3 tablespoons powdered sugar
1½ teaspoons honey
1 large egg white

{ fyi }

Focaccia is a fashionable Italian flatbread, often enjoyed by children as a snack. The dough is usually shaped by hand and topped with seasonings and other ingredients, such as olive oil, that preserve the moisture of the bread.

1. Combine first 3 ingredients in a small saucepan; bring to a boil over medium-high heat. Cook 1 minute or until golden. Drain nut mixture through a fine sieve into a bowl, reserving oil. Toss nuts with ⅛ teaspoon salt and red pepper in a bowl.
2. Combine milk, granulated sugar, and yeast in a large bowl; let stand 5 minutes or until bubbly. Weigh or lightly spoon flour into dry measuring cups; level with a knife. Add reserved oil, 5.7 ounces flour (about 1¼ cups), 1 teaspoon salt, and egg yolk to yeast mixture; beat with a mixer at low speed until combined. Gradually add remaining 9 ounces flour (about 2 cups) to oil mixture; beat at low speed until a soft, elastic dough forms (about 3 minutes). Press dough into a jelly-roll pan coated with 1½ tablespoons oil. Cover with plastic wrap; let rise in a warm place (85°) for 40 minutes or until almost doubled in size.
3. Preheat oven to 350°.
4. Press dough gently with fingertips. Combine remaining 1½ teaspoons oil, powdered sugar, honey, and egg white, and stir with a whisk until smooth. Gently brush dough with half of egg white mixture. Bake at 350° for 20 minutes. Remove pan from oven. Brush top of bread with remaining egg white mixture; sprinkle with almond mixture. Bake an additional 10 minutes or until golden brown. Remove from pan; cool 10 minutes on a wire rack. Yield: 24 servings (serving size: 1 [2½-inch-square] piece).

CALORIES 137; FAT 7.1g (sat 1g, mono 4.9g, poly 0.9g); PROTEIN 2.9g; CARB 15.5g; FIBER 0.8g; CHOL 8mg; IRON 1mg; SODIUM 119mg; CALC 21mg

Brioche Rolls

Meringue-Topped
Cranberry Curd
Tart, page 50

pies, pastries & cheesecakes

Creamy, fruity, or laced with chocolate, these classic dessert offerings are guaranteed to elicit raves from family and friends.

Plum Galette with Armagnac Cream **42**

Vanilla-Bourbon Pumpkin Tart **42**

Apple Tarte Tatin **45**

Pear Tarte Tatin **45**

Maple-Walnut Apple Crisp **46**

Roasted Pear Crème Brûlée Tart **46**

Chocolate Walnut Tart **49**

Caramel Apple Pie **49**

Meringue-Topped Cranberry Curd Tart **50**

Rustic Apple Tart **50**

Mexican Chocolate Cream Pie **53**

Coconut Cream Pie **53**

Key Lime Pie **54**

Lemon Cream Pie **54**

New York Cheesecake **57**

Baklava **57**

Cranberry Swirl Cheesecake **58**

Chocolate Chip Cannoli **58**

Plum Galette with Armagnac Cream ▶

Hands-on time: 45 min. Total time: 2 hr. 15 min. Armagnac, one of the world's two great brandies (the other being cognac), hails from southwest France. It is often paired with plums, both fresh and dried.

Galette:
6 ounces all-purpose flour (about 1⅓ cups)
3 tablespoons whole-wheat pastry flour
2 teaspoons granulated sugar
¼ teaspoon salt
8 tablespoons chilled butter, cut into small pieces
¼ cup ice water
3 pounds ripe plums, quartered
9 tablespoons brown sugar, divided
¼ cup Armagnac or cognac
1 vanilla bean, halved
1 (1-ounce) slice whole-wheat bread
2 tablespoons butter, melted
Cream:
1 cup light sour cream
⅓ cup powdered sugar
2 tablespoons whole milk
2 tablespoons Armagnac or cognac
1 teaspoon vanilla extract

1. To prepare galette, weigh or lightly spoon flours into dry measuring cups; level with a knife. Combine flours, granulated sugar, and salt in a medium bowl, and cut in butter with a pastry blender or 2 knives until mixture resembles coarse meal. Add ice water; stir just until moist. Pat dough into a 7-inch circle on plastic wrap; cover. Chill for 15 minutes.
2. Combine plums, ½ cup brown sugar, ¼ cup Armagnac, and vanilla bean in a large skillet over medium heat; cook 10 minutes or until plums are tender, stirring occasionally. Cool to room temperature.
3. Preheat oven to 300°.
4. Tear bread into 1-inch pieces. Place on baking sheet; bake at 300° for 30 minutes or until dry and golden. Place bread in a food processor; process until coarse crumbs measure ¼ cup.
5. Increase oven temperature to 425°.
6. Unwrap and place the dough on a baking sheet. Roll dough into a 15-inch circle; sprinkle dough with breadcrumbs, leaving a 2-inch border. Arrange plum mixture over crumbs. Fold edges of dough over plum mixture (dough will only partially cover plum mixture). Brush dough edges and top of fruit with melted butter; sprinkle with remaining 1 tablespoon brown sugar. Bake at 425° for 15 minutes. Reduce oven temperature to 375° (do not remove galette from oven); bake an additional 20 minutes or until bubbly and edges are golden. Cool 5 minutes on pan; loosen galette from pan. Cool 30 minutes on pan.
7. To prepare cream, combine sour cream and remaining ingredients in a small bowl, stirring with a whisk. Serve over galette slices. Yield: 12 servings (serving size: 1 galette slice and 1½ teaspoons cream).

CALORIES 277; **FAT** 11.4g (sat 7.4g, mono 2.5g, poly 0.4g); **PROTEIN** 4g; **CARB** 35.9g; **FIBER** 3g; **CHOL** 25mg; **IRON** 1.2mg; **SODIUM** 149mg; **CALC** 34mg

Vanilla-Bourbon Pumpkin Tart ▼

Hands-on time: 30 min. Total time: 5 hrs. 13 min. Graham crackers and pecans encrust the spirited, spiced filling. Dollop each serving with sweetened whipped cream.

Crust:
¾ cup graham cracker crumbs (about 5 cookie sheets)
1 tablespoon finely chopped pecans
1 teaspoon granulated sugar

1 tablespoon butter, melted
Cooking spray
Filling:
1 cup (8 ounces) ⅓-less-fat cream cheese, softened
½ cup granulated sugar
¼ cup packed light brown sugar
1 (15-ounce) can unsweetened pumpkin
2 large eggs
2 tablespoons bourbon
2 teaspoons vanilla extract
½ teaspoon salt
½ teaspoon ground cinnamon
¼ teaspoon ground nutmeg
⅛ teaspoon ground allspice
Remaining ingredients:
⅓ cup cold heavy cream
2 teaspoons powdered sugar

1. Preheat oven to 350°.
2. To prepare crust, combine the first 3 ingredients in a bowl. Drizzle butter over crumb mixture; stir with a fork. Firmly press into bottom and 1 inch up sides of a 9-inch springform pan coated with cooking spray. Bake at 350° for 8 minutes or until lightly browned; cool on a wire rack.
3. To prepare filling, beat cream cheese, ½ cup granulated sugar, and brown sugar in a large bowl with a mixer at medium speed until smooth. Add pumpkin and eggs; beat until combined, scraping sides of bowl as needed. Add bourbon and the next 5 ingredients (through ground allspice); beat 1 minute or until combined. Pour cheese mixture into prepared pan. Place pan in a large roasting pan; add hot water to pan to a depth of 1 inch. Bake at 350° for 35 minutes or until center barely moves when side of pan is tapped. Cool completely on wire rack. Cover and refrigerate at least 4 hours or overnight. Place cream and powdered sugar in a small bowl; beat with a mixer at high speed until stiff peaks form. Serve sweetened whipped cream with tart. Yield: 8 servings (serving size: 1 wedge and about 1 tablespoon whipped cream).

CALORIES 284; **FAT** 14.1g (sat 7.8g, mono 4.4g, poly 0.9g); **PROTEIN** 6.4g; **CARB** 32.2g; **FIBER** 2.7g; **CHOL** 90mg; **IRON** 1.1mg; **SODIUM** 356mg; **CALC** 54mg

Fruits of the season
star in these luscious
showstopping tarts.

Apple Tarte Tatin ▶

Hands-on time: 45 min. Total time: 2 hr. 20 min.
Caramel-bathed apples nestle in a tender
crust, while crème fraîche lends a little French
tang to this fall classic.

6.75 ounces all-purpose flour
   (about 1½ cups)
¼ teaspoon salt
6 tablespoons butter, softened
6 tablespoons water, divided
1 large egg
1 cup sugar
2 pounds Golden Delicious apples,
   peeled, cored, and quartered
   (about 6 small)
¼ teaspoon ground cinnamon
10 teaspoons crème fraîche

1. Preheat oven to 400°.
2. Weigh or lightly spoon flour into dry measuring cups; level with a knife. Place flour and salt in a medium bowl; cut in butter with a pastry blender or 2 knives until mixture resembles coarse meal. Combine 2 tablespoons water and egg, stirring with a whisk. Add egg mixture to flour mixture, stirring just until moist. Turn dough out onto a large piece of heavy-duty plastic wrap; knead lightly 5 times (dough will be sticky). Pat dough into a disk. Cover with additional plastic wrap; chill 30 minutes.
3. Combine remaining ¼ cup water and sugar in a 9-inch cast-iron skillet over medium-high heat. Cook 10 minutes or until golden, stirring just until sugar dissolves. Remove from heat; gently stir in small circles to evenly distribute cooked sugar. Let stand 5 minutes.
4. Arrange apple quarters tightly in a circular pattern over sugar in pan, beginning at the outside edge. Cut 2 apple quarters in half, and arrange, points up, in center of pan. Place pan over medium heat; cook 20 minutes (do not stir), pressing apples slightly to extract juices. Remove from heat; let stand for 10 minutes. Sprinkle cinnamon over apples.
5. Remove plastic wrap covering dough. Turn dough out onto a lightly floured surface; roll dough into an 11-inch circle. Place over apple mixture, fitting dough between apples and skillet. Bake at 400° for 20 minutes or until

A delicious syrup glazes the tart when it is inverted.

lightly browned. Cool 10 minutes. Invert tart onto a plate. Serve with crème fraîche. Yield: 10 servings (serving size: 1 slice tart and 1 teaspoon crème fraîche).

CALORIES 275; FAT 9.3g (sat 5.6g, mono 2g, poly 0.4g); PROTEIN 3.1g; CARB 46.3g; FIBER 1.7g; CHOL 44mg; IRON 1.1mg; SODIUM 115mg; CALC 13mg

Pear Tarte Tatin ◀

Hands-on time: 40 min. Total time: 1 hr.

2 tablespoons butter, divided
½ cup sugar, divided
4 peeled ripe Anjou pears, cored and
   halved lengthwise
1 tablespoon canola oil
4 (14 x 9-inch) sheets frozen phyllo
   dough, thawed
3 tablespoons crème fraîche

1. Preheat oven to 400°.
2. Coat a 10-inch cast-iron skillet with 1½ tablespoons butter. Sprinkle 6 tablespoons sugar into pan. Arrange 7 pear halves, cut sides up, in a circle in pan; place remaining pear half in center. Cover pan; place over medium-low heat. Cook, without stirring, for 15 minutes or until sugar mixture is bubbly and caramelized. Place pan in oven. Bake at 400° for 5 minutes.
3. Place 1½ teaspoons butter and oil in a bowl. Microwave at HIGH for 30 seconds or until butter melts. Lay 1 phyllo sheet horizontally on a flat work surface; brush lightly with butter mixture. Sprinkle 2 teaspoons sugar evenly over phyllo. Place next phyllo sheet vertically on top of first. Repeat procedure twice with remaining butter mixture, sugar, and phyllo, ending with phyllo. Fold edges to form a 9-inch circle.
4. Place phyllo circle in pan over pears, pressing gently. Bake at 400° for 16 minutes or until filling is bubbly and crust is browned. Remove tart from oven, and let stand for 5 minutes. Place a plate upside-down on top of pan, and invert tart onto plate. Cut tart into 6 wedges. Top each wedge with 1½ teaspoons crème fraîche. Yield: 6 servings.

CALORIES 258; FAT 10.3g (sat 4.4g, mono 2.9g, poly 1g); PROTEIN 2g; CARB 41.7g; FIBER 3g; CHOL 17mg; IRON 0.5mg; SODIUM 79mg; CALC 70mg

Maple-Walnut Apple Crisp ▶

Hands-on time: 20 min. Total time: 1 hr. 5 min.
Add a small scoop of low-fat vanilla ice cream
to this dessert when it's warm from the oven.

1.5 ounces all-purpose flour
(about ⅓ cup)
½ cup packed light brown sugar
⅓ cup regular oats
¼ teaspoon ground cinnamon
¼ cup chilled butter, cut into small
pieces
3 tablespoons chopped walnuts
7 cups sliced peeled Rome apple
(about 3 pounds)
¼ cup maple syrup
½ teaspoon ground cinnamon

1. Preheat oven to 375°.
2. Weigh or lightly spoon flour into a
dry measuring cup; level with a knife.
Combine flour, sugar, oats, and ¼
teaspoon cinnamon in a medium bowl,
and cut in butter with a pastry blender
or 2 knives until mixture is crumbly.
Stir in walnuts.
3. Combine apple and remaining
ingredients in a large bowl; toss well.
Spoon apple mixture into an 8-inch
square glass or ceramic baking dish
or 1½-quart casserole. Sprinkle with
crumb mixture. Bake at 375° for 45
minutes or until golden brown. Serve
warm. Yield: 6 servings.

CALORIES 313; **FAT** 10.7g (sat 5.2g, mono 2.5g, poly
2.2g); **PROTEIN** 2.4g; **CARB** 55.5g; **FIBER** 3g; **CHOL**
20mg; **IRON** 1.1mg; **SODIUM** 61mg; **CALC** 42mg

{ fyi }

You may find eight varieties of
apples in your supermarket
and a dozen or more in a big
farmers' market, but they
perform very differently when
cooked. Mild-tasting Rome,
sugary-sweet and juicy Honey-
crisp, tart Jonagold, and
slightly acidic Spartan are a
few that are good for baking.

Roasted Pear Crème Brûlée Tart ▶

Hands-on time: 45 min. Total time: 5 hr. 20 min.

Pastry:
1 tablespoon granulated sugar
¼ teaspoon salt
4 ounces all-purpose flour (about ¾
cup plus 2 tablespoons)
¼ cup chilled butter, cut into small
pieces
2 tablespoons ice water
Cooking spray
Pastry cream:
¼ cup packed brown sugar
3 tablespoons all-purpose flour
⅛ teaspoon salt
2 cups 2% reduced-fat milk
1 (4-inch) piece vanilla bean, split
lengthwise
1 large egg, lightly beaten
Topping:
1 teaspoon fresh lemon juice
¼ teaspoon ground cinnamon
⅛ teaspoon ground nutmeg
2 medium pears, peeled, cored, and
halved
⅓ cup granulated sugar

1. Preheat oven to 450°.
2. To prepare pastry, place the first 3
ingredients in a food processor; pulse
to combine. Add butter; pulse 10
times or until mixture resembles
coarse meal. With processor on,
slowly add 2 tablespoons ice water
through food chute, processing just
until dough starts to come together.
Turn dough out onto a piece of plastic
wrap; press into a disk. Cover and
chill 10 minutes in the freezer. Place
dough between 2 sheets of plastic
wrap, and roll dough into a 10-inch
circle. Fit dough into a 9-inch round
removable-bottom tart pan coated
with cooking spray; pierce dough with
a fork. Bake at 450° for 10 minutes or
until lightly browned. Cool completely
on a wire rack.
3. To prepare pastry cream, combine
brown sugar, 3 tablespoons flour,
and ⅛ teaspoon salt in a medium
heavy saucepan. Gradually add milk,
stirring with a whisk. Scrape seeds
from vanilla bean; add seeds and bean
to milk mixture. Cook over medium-
high heat until thick and bubbly
(about 5 minutes), stirring constantly.
Place egg in a large bowl. Gradually
stir hot milk mixture into egg. Return
milk mixture to pan; cook 2 minutes
or until mixture reaches 185° and
coats the back of a spoon, stirring
constantly. Discard vanilla bean.
Spread pastry cream onto a baking
sheet; cover entire surface with plastic
wrap. Refrigerate 20 minutes or until
chilled. Spread pastry cream evenly
into tart shell; cover and chill at least
2 hours or until set.
4. To prepare topping, combine lemon
juice, cinnamon, nutmeg, and pears;
toss well to coat. Place the pears, cut
side down, in an 11 x 7–inch baking
dish coated with cooking spray. Bake
at 450° for 45 minutes or until pears
are tender. Cool completely, and
thinly slice. Place on paper towels; pat
dry with additional paper towels.
Arrange the pear slices spoke-like over
the pastry cream. Cover and chill at
least 30 minutes.
5. Sprinkle ⅓ cup granulated sugar
evenly over pears, leaving a ½-inch
border. Holding a kitchen blowtorch
about 2 inches from the top of custard,
heat the sugar, moving the torch back
and forth, until the sugar is melted
and caramelized (about 3 minutes).
Serve immediately. Yield: 8 servings
(serving size: 1 wedge).

CALORIES 241; **FAT** 7.6g (sat 4.5g, mono 2.1g, poly 0.4g);
PROTEIN 4.8g; **CARB** 39.3g; **FIBER** 1.8g; **CHOL** 42mg;
IRON 1.2mg; **SODIUM** 194mg; **CALC** 92mg

Chocolate Walnut Tart ◄

Hands-on time: 13 min. Total time: 1 hr. 10 min.
A riff on the classic pecan pie, this dessert is rich, chocolaty, and a little fancier with its freestanding fluted sides. Of course, you can use a 9-inch pie plate if you don't have a tart pan with a removable bottom.

1/3 cup packed brown sugar
2 tablespoons all-purpose flour
1/4 teaspoon salt
1/2 cup light-colored corn syrup
2 tablespoons butter, at room temperature
4 ounces bittersweet chocolate, finely chopped
1 cup walnut halves
1/2 teaspoon vanilla extract
3 large eggs, lightly beaten
1/2 (14.1-ounce) package refrigerated pie dough (such as Pillsbury)
Cooking spray

1. Arrange 1 rack in lower third of oven. Preheat oven to 350°.
2. Combine brown sugar, flour, and salt in a medium heavy saucepan over medium heat, stirring well with a whisk. Stir in corn syrup, and bring mixture to a boil. Cook 1 minute, stirring occasionally until sugar dissolves. Remove from heat. Add butter and chocolate; stir with a whisk until smooth. Cool to room temperature; stir in walnuts, vanilla, and eggs.
3. Fit the pie dough into a 9-inch round removable-bottom tart pan coated with cooking spray, pressing dough into the bottom and up the sides of the pan.
4. Spoon walnut mixture into prepared crust. Bake on bottom oven rack at 350° for 33 minutes or until set. Cool for 20 minutes in pan on a wire rack. Remove sides of tart pan; slide tart onto a serving platter. Cut into wedges. Yield: 12 servings (serving size: 1 wedge).

CALORIES 292; **FAT** 18.3g (sat 5.9g, mono 5.1g, poly 6.2g); **PROTEIN** 4.2g; **CARB** 32.3g; **FIBER** 1.4g; **CHOL** 60mg; **IRON** 0.9mg; **SODIUM** 165mg; **CALC** 24mg

Caramel Apple Pie ▲

Hands-on time: 40 min. Total time: 2 hr. 29 min.

Topping:
1.1 ounces all-purpose flour (about 1/4 cup)
1/4 cup packed light brown sugar
2 tablespoons chilled butter, cut into small pieces
Crust:
5.6 ounces all-purpose flour (about 1 1/4 cups)
1/4 teaspoon salt
3 tablespoons chilled butter, cut into small pieces
2 tablespoons chilled vegetable shortening, cut into small pieces
3 tablespoons ice water
Cooking spray
Filling:
1/4 cup granulated sugar
2 tablespoons cornstarch
4 cups thinly sliced peeled Granny Smith apple (about 1 1/4 pounds)
3 cups thinly sliced peeled Fuji apple (about 1 pound)
Caramel sauce:
1/2 cup fat-free caramel sundae syrup
1/8 teaspoon kosher salt

1. To prepare topping, weigh or lightly spoon 1.1 ounces (about 1/4 cup) flour into a dry measuring cup; level with a knife. Combine flour, brown sugar, and 2 tablespoons butter in a food processor; pulse 10 times or until crumbly. Transfer topping to a bowl; cover and chill.
2. To prepare crust, weigh or lightly spoon 5.6 ounces (about 1 1/4 cups) flour into dry measuring cups; level with a knife. Combine flour and 1/4 teaspoon salt in a food processor; pulse 2 times or until combined. Add 3 tablespoons butter and shortening; pulse 4 times or until mixture resembles coarse meal. With processor on, add 3 tablespoons water through food chute, processing just until combined (do not form a ball). Press mixture gently into a 4-inch circle on plastic wrap; cover and chill 15 minutes. Slightly overlap 2 sheets of plastic wrap on a slightly damp surface. Unwrap dough, and place on plastic wrap. Cover with 2 additional sheets of overlapping plastic wrap. Roll dough into an 11-inch circle. Freeze dough 5 minutes or until plastic wrap can be easily removed.
3. Preheat oven to 375°.
4. Discard top 2 sheets of plastic wrap; let dough stand 1 minute or until pliable. Fit dough, plastic-wrap side up, into a 9-inch pie plate coated with cooking spray. Discard plastic wrap. Press dough into bottom and up sides of pan. Fold edges under; flute.
5. To prepare filling, combine granulated sugar and cornstarch in a bowl; stir with a whisk. Add apples; toss to combine. Arrange apple mixture in crust, mounding slightly in the center. Bake at 375° for 25 minutes. Remove from oven; sprinkle evenly with topping. Bake at 375° for 25 additional minutes or until golden. Cool on a wire rack 20 minutes.
6. To prepare sauce, combine caramel syrup and salt. Slice pie into 12 wedges; serve with sauce. Yield: 12 servings (serving size: 1 pie wedge and 2 teaspoons sauce).

CALORIES 280; **FAT** 8.4g (sat 4.5g, mono 2.2g, poly 1g); **PROTEIN** 2.2g; **CARB** 49.6g; **FIBER** 1.7g; **CHOL** 15mg; **IRON** 1.1mg; **SODIUM** 169mg; **CALC** 14mg

{ fyi }

To make a fluted edge, tuck the extra dough under the outside edges. Pinch dough with thumb and index finger of one hand. Press inward with the thumb of your other hand.

Meringue-Topped Cranberry Curd Tart

Hands-on time: 1 hr. Total time: 2 hr. 3 min.
Making perfect pastry depends mostly on how well you coat flour proteins with fat—more difficult in a low-fat recipe. You want to leave small clumps of fat in the dough (here, from vegetable shortening) so they'll melt during cooking and give off steam, creating luscious layers. Meanwhile, we melted the butter so it would coat more than it would in solid form. Tart shown on page 40.

Crust:
5 ounces all-purpose flour (about 1¼ cups)
1 tablespoon sugar
¼ teaspoon salt
¼ teaspoon baking powder
¼ cup vegetable shortening
¼ cup boiling water
4 teaspoons butter, melted
Cooking spray
Filling:
1 (12-ounce) package fresh cranberries
1 cup sugar, divided
¾ cup water, divided
⅛ teaspoon salt
¼ cup cornstarch
2 large egg yolks
2 tablespoons butter, softened
Meringue:
3 large egg whites
⅛ teaspoon salt
½ cup sugar
¼ cup water

1. Weigh or lightly spoon flour into dry measuring cups; level with a knife. Combine first 4 ingredients in a bowl; cut in shortening with a pastry blender until mixture resembles coarse meal. Make a well in center of flour mixture. Combine ¼ cup boiling water and melted butter in a bowl. Pour butter mixture into center of well. Gently draw flour mixture into butter mixture until moist clumps form. Press dough

PREP POINTER

Vegetable shortening creates flaky layers in the crust. Overworking the dough will make it tough.

into a 4-inch circle on plastic wrap; cover. Chill for 30 minutes.
2. Preheat oven to 400°.
3. Unwrap dough; place between 2 sheets of plastic wrap. Roll dough into an 11-inch circle. Remove top sheet of plastic wrap. Fit dough, plastic wrap side up, into a 9-inch round tart pan coated with cooking spray. Remove plastic wrap. Press dough into bottom and up sides of pan; fold excess crust back in and press. Pierce bottom and sides of dough lightly with a fork; freeze 10 minutes. Line bottom of dough with foil; arrange pie weights on foil. Bake at 400° for 18 minutes. Remove foil and pie weights. Bake 15 minutes or until lightly browned. Cool on a wire rack.
4. Combine cranberries, ½ cup sugar, ¼ cup water, and ⅛ teaspoon salt in a medium saucepan. Cook over medium-high heat 10 minutes or until cranberries burst. Combine ½ cup sugar, ½ cup water, cornstarch, and egg yolks in a small bowl; stir with a whisk until smooth. Gradually add 1 cup hot cranberry mixture to egg mixture, stirring constantly. Return egg mixture to pan. Cook until a thermometer registers 160°, stirring constantly.
5. Place a food mill or fine sieve over a large bowl. Pour cranberry mixture into food mill, and press through. Discard solids. Add 2 tablespoons butter; stir. Spoon into baked crust. Cover and chill.
6. Preheat broiler.
7. Place egg whites and ⅛ teaspoon salt in a large bowl; beat with a mixer at high speed until soft peaks form. Combine ½ cup sugar and ¼ cup water in a small saucepan; bring to a boil. Cook, without stirring, until candy thermometer registers 238°. Gradually pour hot sugar syrup into egg white mixture, beating until stiff peaks form. Spread meringue over cranberry curd.
8. Broil 30 seconds or until meringue is lightly browned. Yield: 12 servings (serving size: 1 wedge).

CALORIES 245; FAT 8.1g (sat 3.8g, mono 2.3g, poly 1.5g); PROTEIN 2.7g; CARB 41.1g; FIBER 1.7g; CHOL 43mg; IRON 0.7mg; SODIUM 147mg; CALC 15mg

Rustic Apple Tart ▶

Hands-on time: 1 hr. Total time: 1 hr. 45 min.

2 tablespoons unsalted butter
¼ cup packed brown sugar
2 tablespoons granulated sugar
4½ cups sliced peeled Golden Delicious apple (about 1½ pounds)
4½ cups sliced peeled Granny Smith apple (about 1½ pounds)
2 teaspoons fresh lemon juice
1 teaspoon ground cinnamon
¼ teaspoon ground nutmeg
½ (14.1-ounce) package refrigerated pie dough (such as Pillsbury)
1 teaspoon ice water
1 teaspoon granulated sugar
1 tablespoon apricot preserves
1 teaspoon water

1. Melt butter in a large skillet over medium-high heat. Add brown sugar and 2 tablespoons granulated sugar; cook 2 minutes or until sugars dissolve. Stir in apples and next 3 ingredients (through ground nutmeg). Cover, reduce heat, and cook 20 minutes or until apples are tender, stirring occasionally. Remove from heat; cool to room temperature.
2. Preheat oven to 400°. Set oven rack to lowest third of oven.
3. Place dough on a piece of parchment paper. Roll dough into a 14-inch circle. Place dough and parchment paper on a baking sheet. Arrange cooled apples in center of dough, leaving a 2-inch border. Fold the edges of dough toward center, pressing gently to seal (dough will only partially cover the apple mixture). Brush dough with 1 teaspoon ice water; sprinkle evenly with 1 teaspoon granulated sugar. Bake the tart at 400° for 45 minutes or until golden brown.
4. Place apricot preserves and 1 teaspoon water in a small microwave-safe bowl. Microwave at HIGH for 30 seconds or until bubbly. Brush the mixture over warm tart. Cut into wedges, and serve warm or at room temperature. Yield: 8 servings (serving size: 1 wedge).

CALORIES 241; FAT 10g (sat 4.8g, mono 2.7g, poly 0.8g); PROTEIN 1.4g; CARB 40.1g; FIBER 1.8g; CHOL 10.6mg; IRON 0.2mg; SODIUM 140mg; CALC 16mg

Mexican Chocolate Cream Pie ◄

Hands-on time: 35 min. Total time: 4 hr.
Ground red pepper adds a subtle but distinct
kick to the pie, while instant espresso powder
intensifies the flavor. Omit either or both if
you prefer a standard chocolate cream pie.

Crust:
1½ cups graham cracker crumbs
   (about 10 cookie sheets), divided
2 tablespoons sugar
1 teaspoon ground cinnamon
⅛ teaspoon salt
2 tablespoons egg white
2 tablespoons butter, melted
Cooking spray
Filling:
½ cup sugar
2 tablespoons cornstarch
1 tablespoon unsweetened cocoa
¼ teaspoon instant espresso powder
⅛ teaspoon salt
⅛ teaspoon ground red pepper
1 large egg
1 large egg yolk
1¾ cups 2% reduced-fat milk
2 ounces dark chocolate, chopped
1½ cups frozen reduced-calorie
   whipped topping, thawed

1. Preheat oven to 375°.
2. To prepare crust, reserve 1 tablespoon crumbs for topping. Combine remaining crumbs, 2 tablespoons sugar, cinnamon, and ⅛ teaspoon salt in a bowl, stirring well. Stir in egg white and butter. Press crumb mixture into bottom and up sides of a 9-inch pie plate coated with cooking spray. Bake at 375° for 9 minutes or until lightly toasted; cool completely on a wire rack.
3. To prepare filling, combine ½ cup sugar and next 7 ingredients (through egg yolk) in a bowl, stirring well with a whisk. Place milk in a medium heavy saucepan over medium-high heat; cook until milk reaches 180° or until tiny bubbles form around edge (do not boil). Gradually add hot milk to egg mixture, stirring constantly with a whisk. Return milk mixture to pan; cook over medium heat 10 minutes or until thick and bubbly, stirring constantly. Remove from heat. Add chocolate; stir until smooth.
4. Place pan in a large ice-filled bowl for 10 minutes or until mixture cools, stirring occasionally. Spoon filling into crust, and cover surface of filling with plastic wrap. Chill 3 hours or until set; remove plastic wrap. Spread whipped topping over filling; sprinkle with reserved cracker crumbs. Yield: 8 servings (serving size: 1 slice).

CALORIES 278; FAT 10.3g (sat 5.8g, mono 2.8g, poly 1g); PROTEIN 5g; CARB 42.1g; FIBER 1.3g; CHOL 57mg; IRON 1.5mg; SODIUM 231mg; CALC 81mg

Coconut Cream Pie ▼

Hands-on time: 25 min. Total time: 4 hr.

½ (14.1-ounce) package refrigerated
   pie dough (such as Pillsbury)
Cooking spray
2 cups 1% low-fat milk
1 cup half-and-half
1½ cups flaked sweetened coconut
1 vanilla bean, split lengthwise
⅔ cup sugar
⅓ cup cornstarch
¼ teaspoon salt
4 large egg yolks
2 tablespoons butter
3 large egg whites, at room
   temperature
½ teaspoon cream of tartar
½ cup sugar
¼ cup water
¼ cup flaked sweetened coconut,
   toasted

1. Preheat oven to 425°.
2. Fit dough into a 9-inch pie plate coated with cooking spray. Fold edges under; flute. Line dough with foil; arrange pie weights or dried beans on foil. Bake at 425° for 10 minutes; remove weights and foil, and bake an additional 10 minutes or until golden. Cool completely on a wire rack.
3. Combine milk and the half-and-half in a medium saucepan over medium heat. Add 1½ cups coconut. Scrape seeds from vanilla bean; stir seeds and pod into milk mixture. Bring mixture to a simmer; immediately remove from heat. Cover and let stand 15 minutes. Strain through a cheesecloth-lined sieve into a bowl. Gather edges of cheesecloth; squeeze over bowl to release moisture. Discard solids.
4. Combine ⅔ cup sugar, cornstarch, salt, and egg yolks in a large bowl, stirring with a whisk. Gradually add milk mixture to egg yolk mixture, stirring constantly. Return milk mixture to pan, and bring to a boil, whisking constantly. Remove from heat. Add butter, and whisk until smooth. Place pan in a large ice-filled bowl for 6 minutes, stirring to cool. Pour into prepared crust. Cover and chill at least 1 hour.
5. Place 3 egg whites and cream of tartar in a large bowl; beat with a mixer at high speed until soft peaks form. Combine ½ cup sugar and ¼ cup water in a saucepan; bring to a boil. Cook, without stirring, until candy thermometer registers 250°. Pour hot sugar syrup in a thin stream over egg whites, beating at high speed until thick. Spread meringue over pie. Cover and refrigerate at least 2 hours. Top with toasted coconut before serving. Yield: 12 servings (serving size: 1 wedge).

CALORIES 266; FAT 11.5g (sat 5.7g, mono 1.3g, poly 0.3g); PROTEIN 4.2g; CARB 36.4g; FIBER 0.3g; CHOL 79mg; IRON 0.4mg; SODIUM 189mg; CALC 79mg

Lemon Cream Pie ◀

Hands-on time: 25 min. Total time: 4 hr.
This lightened classic is sweet-tart perfection
and a delicious ending to any meal.

**1/2 (14.1-ounce) package refrigerated
    pie dough (such as Pillsbury)**
Cooking spray
1/2 cup sugar
**1 tablespoon grated lemon rind,
    divided**
1/4 cup fresh lemon juice
3 tablespoons cornstarch
1/4 teaspoon salt
2 large eggs
1 1/2 cups fat-free milk
**1/4 cup (2 ounces) 1/3-less-fat cream
    cheese, softened**
2 tablespoons butter, softened
**1 1/2 cups frozen fat-free whipped
    topping, thawed**

1. Roll dough into a 12-inch circle; fit into a 9-inch pie plate coated with cooking spray. Fold edges under, and flute. Bake piecrust according to package directions. Cool completely on a wire rack.
2. Combine sugar, 2 1/2 teaspoons rind, and the next 4 ingredients (through eggs) in a large bowl, stirring well. Combine milk and cheese in a medium heavy saucepan over medium-high heat; cook until mixture reaches 180° or until tiny bubbles form around edge (do not boil). Gradually add the hot milk mixture to sugar mixture, stirring constantly with a whisk. Return milk mixture to pan, and cook over medium heat 10 minutes or until thick and bubbly, stirring constantly. Remove from heat; stir in butter.
3. Place pan in a large ice-filled bowl for 10 minutes or until the mixture cools to room temperature, stirring occasionally. Spoon filling into prepared crust, and cover surface of filling with plastic wrap. Chill 3 hours or until set; remove plastic wrap. Spread whipped topping evenly over chilled pie; sprinkle with remaining 1/2 teaspoon lemon rind. Yield: 8 servings (serving size: 1 slice).

CALORIES 264; **FAT** 11.9g (sat 5.9g, mono 3.4g, poly 1.9g); **PROTEIN** 4.6g; **CARB** 34.8g; **FIBER** 0.1g; **CHOL** 61mg; **IRON** 0.3mg; **SODIUM** 296mg; **CALC** 72mg

Key Lime Pie ▶

Hands-on time: 35 min. Total time: 3 hr.
This dessert is best enjoyed the day it's made.

**1 1/2 cups graham cracker crumbs
    (about 10 cookie sheets)**
2 tablespoons butter, melted
4 large egg whites, divided
1 tablespoon water
Cooking spray
2 large eggs
2 large egg yolks
**1/2 cup fresh Key lime juice or fresh
    lime juice (about 6 Key limes)**
**1 (14-ounce) can fat-free sweetened
    condensed milk**
**1 teaspoon grated Key lime or lime
    rind**
1/2 cup sugar
2 1/2 tablespoons water

1. Preheat oven to 350°.
2. Combine crumbs and melted butter in a bowl. Place 1 egg white in a small bowl; stir well with a whisk until foamy. Add 2 tablespoons egg white to graham cracker mixture, tossing well with a fork to combine. Discard remaining beaten egg white. Add 1 tablespoon water to graham cracker mixture; toss gently to coat. Press into bottom and up sides of a 9-inch pie plate coated with cooking spray. (Moisten fingers, if needed, to bring mixture together.) Bake at 350° for 8 minutes. Cool completely on a wire rack.
3. Place 2 eggs and 2 egg yolks in a mixing bowl; beat at medium speed until well blended. Add juice and condensed milk, beating until thick; stir in rind. Spoon into prepared crust. Bake at 350° for 20 minutes or until edges are set (center will set as it chills). Cool completely on a wire rack. Cover loosely. Chill at least 2 hours.
4. Place remaining 3 egg whites in a bowl; beat with a mixer at medium until foamy using clean, dry beaters.
5. Combine sugar and 2 1/2 tablespoons water in a small saucepan; bring to a boil. Cook, without stirring, until a candy thermometer registers 250°. Pour hot sugar syrup in a thin stream over egg whites, beating at high speed 2 minutes or until stiff peaks form. Spread meringue over chilled pie (completely cover pie with meringue).
6. Preheat broiler.
7. Broil pie 1 minute or until meringue is lightly browned. Yield: 8 servings (serving size: 1 slice).

CALORIES 320; **FAT** 6.8g (sat 2.8g, mono 2.3g, poly 1.1g); **PROTEIN** 9g; **CARB** 55.5g; **FIBER** 0.5g; **CHOL** 118mg; **IRON** 1mg; **SODIUM** 214mg; **CALC** 146mg

A spectacular, fluffy meringue tower crowns the sweet-tart lime filling.

New York Cheesecake ◄

Hands-on time: 25 min. Total time: 10 hr. 38 min.
Garnish with fresh blueberries, if desired.

1 cup graham cracker crumbs
  (about 7 cookie sheets)
3 tablespoons sugar
1 large egg white
Cooking spray
1 ounce all-purpose flour (¼ cup)
½ cup 1% low-fat cottage cheese
3 (8-ounce) blocks fat-free cream
  cheese, softened and divided
2 (8-ounce) blocks ⅓-less-fat cream
  cheese, softened
1¾ cups sugar
1½ teaspoons finely grated lemon
  rind
2 tablespoons fresh lemon juice
½ teaspoon vanilla extract
3 large eggs
3 large egg whites

1. Preheat oven to 350°.
2. Combine crumbs, 3 tablespoons sugar, and 1 egg white; toss with a fork until well blended. Lightly coat hands with cooking spray. Press mixture into bottom of a 9-inch springform pan coated with cooking spray. Bake at 350° for 8 minutes; cool on a wire rack. Reduce oven temperature to 325°.
3. Weigh or lightly spoon flour into a dry measuring cup; level with a knife. Combine cottage cheese and 8 ounces fat-free cream cheese in a food processor; process until smooth. Add remaining 16 ounces fat-free cream cheese, ⅓-less-fat cream cheese, and next 4 ingredients (through vanilla extract); process until smooth. Add 3 eggs and 3 egg whites; process until blended. Pour cheese mixture into prepared pan. Bake at 325° for 65 minutes or until almost set (center will not be firm but will set as it chills). Turn oven off; cool cheesecake in closed oven 1 hour. Remove from oven; cool on a wire rack. Cover and chill 8 hours. Yield: 16 servings (serving size: 1 wedge).

CALORIES 259; **FAT** 8g (sat 4.8g, mono 2.5g, poly 0.4g); **PROTEIN** 12.7g; **CARB** 33.9g; **FIBER** 0.2g; **CHOL** 58mg; **IRON** 0.6mg; **SODIUM** 446mg; **CALC** 111mg

Baklava ▲

Hands-on time: 1 hr. Total time: 1 hr. 30 min.
If you can't find unsalted pistachios, substitute salted and omit the ⅛ teaspoon salt. Use a candy thermometer, not the instant-read type, to cook the syrup. The deep amber–colored wildflower honey adds a delicate floral hint.

Syrup:
1½ cups wildflower honey
½ cup water
1 tablespoon fresh lemon juice
3 whole cloves
1 (3-inch) cinnamon stick
Filling:
⅔ cup unsalted pistachios, coarsely
  chopped
½ cup blanched unsalted almonds,
  coarsely chopped
⅓ cup walnuts, coarsely chopped
¼ cup sugar
¾ teaspoon ground cinnamon
¼ teaspoon ground cardamom
⅛ teaspoon salt
Remaining ingredients:
Cooking spray
24 (14 x 9–inch) sheets frozen phyllo
  dough, thawed
1 tablespoon water

1. To prepare syrup, combine honey, ½ cup water, lemon juice, whole cloves, and cinnamon stick in a medium saucepan over low heat; stir until honey is completely dissolved (about 2 minutes). Increase heat to medium; cook, without stirring, until a candy thermometer registers 230° (about 10 minutes). Remove from heat; keep warm. Remove the whole cloves and the cinnamon stick from syrup with a slotted spoon; discard spices.
2. Preheat oven to 350°.
3. To prepare filling, combine chopped pistachios and next 6 ingredients (through salt) in a medium bowl; set the nut mixture aside.
4. Lightly coat a 13 x 9–inch baking dish with cooking spray. Working with 1 phyllo sheet at a time (cover remaining dough to prevent drying), place 1 phyllo sheet lengthwise in bottom of prepared pan, allowing end of sheet to extend over edges of dish; lightly coat with cooking spray. Repeat procedure with 5 phyllo sheets and cooking spray for a total of 6 layers. Sprinkle phyllo evenly with one-third of nut mixture (about ⅔ cup). Repeat procedure with phyllo, cooking spray, and nut mixture 2 more times. Top last layer of nut mixture with remaining 6 sheets phyllo, each one lightly coated with cooking spray. Lightly coat top phyllo sheet with cooking spray; press baklava gently into pan. Sprinkle baklava surface with 1 tablespoon water.
5. Make 3 even lengthwise cuts and 5 even crosswise cuts to form 24 portions using a sharp knife. Bake at 350° for 30 minutes or until phyllo is golden brown. Remove dish from the oven. Drizzle honey mixture evenly over baklava. Cool in pan on a wire rack. Store, covered, at room temperature. Yield: 24 servings (serving size: 1 piece).

CALORIES 155; **FAT** 4.7g (sat 0.5g, mono 1.3g, poly 1.2g); **PROTEIN** 2.5g; **CARB** 27.6g; **FIBER** 1.2g; **CHOL** 0mg; **IRON** 0.8mg; **SODIUM** 71mg; **CALC** 16mg

{ fyi }

Cooking spray is used to coat the delicate sheets of phyllo dough—it's a hands-free method, as opposed to brushing the fragile sheets with melted butter or oil.

Honey graham crackers can be used for the crust.

over crust. Spoon cranberry mixture over filling; swirl together using the tip of a knife. Place springform pan in a 13 x 9–inch metal baking pan. Add hot water to pan to a depth of 2 inches. Bake at 325° for 50 minutes or until center of cheesecake barely moves when pan is touched.

8. Turn oven off. Cool cheesecake in closed oven 30 minutes. Remove cheesecake from oven. Run a knife around outside edge. Cool on a wire rack. Cover and chill 8 hours. Yield: 12 servings (serving size: 1 wedge).

CALORIES 321; FAT 14.1g (sat 6.1g, mono 5g, poly 1.5g); PROTEIN 10g; CARB 37.8g; FIBER 0.9g; CHOL 81mg; IRON 0.5mg; SODIUM 333mg; CALC 81mg

Chocolate Chip Cannoli ▶

Hands-on time: 1 hr. 15 min.
Total time: 1 hr. 30 min.
We prefer the fresh taste of this recipe's homemade ricotta, which can be made up to four days ahead. You can make the shells and the filling ahead of time, and assemble while the espresso brews.

Ricotta:
1 gallon 1% low-fat milk
4 cups low-fat buttermilk
¼ teaspoon kosher salt
⅔ cup granulated sugar
½ teaspoon vanilla extract
6 ounces fromage blanc
Shells:
Cooking spray
⅓ cup granulated sugar
½ teaspoon ground cinnamon
6 (18 x 14–inch) sheets frozen phyllo dough, thawed
3 tablespoons butter, melted
Remaining ingredients:
2 ounces semisweet chocolate, divided
2 tablespoons sifted powdered sugar

1. To prepare ricotta, line a large colander or sieve with 3 layers of dampened cheesecloth, allowing cheesecloth to extend over outside edges of colander, and place colander in a large bowl.
2. Combine milk and buttermilk in a large heavy stockpot. Cook mixture over medium heat until a candy

Cranberry Swirl Cheesecake ▲

Hands-on time: 35 min. Total time: 10 hr. 51 min.
Run a knife or small metal spatula around the outside edge immediately after removing the cake from the oven. This allows the loosened sides to contract and prevents cracking.

4 ounces chocolate graham crackers
3 tablespoons canola oil
Cooking spray
1½ cups fresh cranberries
½ cup sugar
¼ cup Chambord (raspberry liqueur)
3 tablespoons water
1 cup sugar
2 (8-ounce) packages block-style ⅓-less-fat cream cheese, softened
½ cup (4 ounces) block-style fat-free cream cheese, softened
1 cup plain fat-free Greek yogurt
2 teaspoons vanilla extract
⅛ teaspoon salt
3 large eggs
2 large egg whites

1. Preheat oven to 375°.
2. Wrap outside and bottom of a 9-inch springform pan tightly with a double layer of heavy-duty foil.
3. Place crackers in a food processor; process until finely ground. Drizzle with oil; pulse until combined. Press mixture into bottom and ½ inch up sides of prepared pan coated with cooking spray. Bake at 375° for 8 minutes; cool on a wire rack.
4. Reduce oven temperature to 325°.
5. Place cranberries, sugar, liqueur, and water in a saucepan; boil. Cook 8 minutes or until cranberries pop and mixture is syrupy. Cool 20 minutes. Place mixture in a food processor; process 1 minute or until smooth.
6. Combine 1 cup sugar and cheeses in a large bowl; beat with a mixer at medium speed until smooth. Beat in yogurt, vanilla, and salt. Add whole eggs, 1 at a time, beating well after each addition.
7. Place 2 egg whites in a medium bowl; beat with a mixer at high speed until soft peaks form using clean, dry beaters. Fold beaten egg whites into cream cheese mixture. Pour filling

thermometer reaches 170°, gently stirring constantly. As soon as the milk mixture reaches 170°, stop stirring (whey and curds will separate at this point). Continue to cook, without stirring, until the thermometer reaches 190°. (Be sure not to stir, or curds that have formed will break apart). Immediately remove pan from heat. (Bottom of pan may be slightly scorched.) Pour milk mixture into cheesecloth-lined colander. Drain over bowl for 5 minutes, and discard liquid (whey). Gather edges of cheesecloth together; tie securely. Hang cheesecloth bundle from kitchen faucet, and drain 12 minutes or just until whey stops dripping. Scrape ricotta into a medium bowl. Sprinkle with salt, and toss gently with a fork to combine. Cool to room temperature.

3. Add ⅔ cup granulated sugar, vanilla extract, and fromage blanc to ricotta; beat with a mixer at medium speed until combined. Cover mixture, and refrigerate.

4. Preheat oven to 375°.

5. To prepare shells, cut out 12 (12 x 4–inch) pieces of heavy-duty aluminum foil. Using your index fingers as a guide, loosely roll up each foil piece, jelly-roll fashion, to form a cylinder with a 1-inch opening. Lightly coat outside of cylinders with cooking spray. Combine ⅓ cup granulated sugar and ½ teaspoon cinnamon in a small bowl.

6. Place 1 phyllo sheet on a large cutting board or work surface (cover the remaining dough to prevent drying); lightly brush with butter. Sprinkle evenly with 2 teaspoons sugar mixture. Repeat layers once. Cut phyllo stack lengthwise into 4 equal strips. Place a foil cylinder at bottom of 1 phyllo strip; roll up, jelly-roll fashion, around cylinder. Lightly coat with cooking spray. Place on a parchment paper–

QUICK TIP
To save time, substitute 4 cups part-skim ricotta for homemade, and proceed to step 3 in the recipe.

{ fyi }

Our version of the Sicilian sweet has all the classic's crunch and creaminess— crispy, lightly sweetened shells filled with homemade ricotta and chopped chocolate—with less than half the calories and one third of the saturated fat.

lined baking sheet. Repeat procedure with remaining phyllo, butter, sugar mixture, and foil cylinders. Bake at 375° for 12 minutes or until lightly browned; cool completely on a wire rack. Carefully remove foil cylinders

from phyllo shells by twisting ends of foil in opposite directions and gently pulling foil from shells.

7. Finely chop 1½ ounces chocolate. Combine ricotta mixture and chopped chocolate in a bowl. Transfer mixture to a large zip-top plastic bag; snip off ½ inch of 1 corner of bag. Pipe ricotta mixture evenly into each of 12 prepared shells (about ⅓ cup each). Grate remaining ½ ounce chocolate. Dust cannoli evenly with powdered sugar and grated chocolate; serve immediately. Yield: 12 servings (serving size: 1 cannoli).

CALORIES 340; FAT 12g (sat 7.4g, mono 2.7g, poly 0.4g); PROTEIN 13.7g; CARB 45.5g; FIBER 0.5g; CHOL 26mg; IRON 1mg; SODIUM 401mg; CALC 506mg

Chopped chocolate has richer flavor than minichips.

Pine Nut Cookies,
page 62

cookies, brownies & bars

Whether for a cookie exchange, school function, or family snack, these crowd-pleasing sweet treats are the kind you'll bake over and over again.

Ginger-Lemon Pinwheel Cookies ▶

Hands-on time: 45 min. Total time: 2 hr. 20 min.

Ginger dough:
¼ cup unsalted butter, softened
⅓ cup packed dark brown sugar
¼ cup molasses
1 large egg yolk
6 ounces all-purpose flour
(about 1⅓ cups)
¾ teaspoon ground ginger
¾ teaspoon ground cinnamon
¼ teaspoon salt
⅛ teaspoon ground nutmeg
Dash of ground allspice
Lemon dough:
5 tablespoons unsalted butter,
softened
⅔ cup granulated sugar
1 large egg white
2 teaspoons grated lemon rind
¾ teaspoon vanilla extract
6 ounces all-purpose flour
(about 1⅓ cups)
¼ teaspoon salt

1. To prepare ginger dough, place ¼ cup butter and brown sugar in a medium bowl; beat with a mixer at medium speed until well combined (about 3 minutes). Add molasses and egg yolk; beat until well blended. Weigh or lightly spoon 6 ounces (about 1⅓ cups) flour into dry measuring cups; level with a knife. Combine 6 ounces flour, ginger, and next 4 ingredients (through allspice); stir with a whisk. Add flour mixture to butter mixture; beat at low speed just until combined. Wrap dough in plastic wrap; chill 30 minutes.
2. To prepare lemon dough, place 5 tablespoons butter and granulated sugar in a medium bowl; beat with a mixer at medium speed until blended (about 3 minutes). Add egg white; beat until blended. Beat in rind and vanilla. Weigh or lightly spoon 6 ounces (about 1⅓ cups) flour into dry measuring cups; level with a knife. Combine 6 ounces flour and ¼ teaspoon salt. Add flour mixture to butter mixture; beat at low speed just until combined. Wrap dough in plastic wrap, and chill 30 minutes.
3. Unwrap ginger dough. Roll ginger

{ fyi }

Keep a log of cookie dough in your refrigerator or freezer, ready to bake—just slice off as many cookies as you want. Each time you slice off a cookie from the log, turn the log one quarter to prevent flattening on one side. If the dough gets soft, chill until slightly firm.

dough between sheets of plastic wrap into a 13 x 8½–inch rectangle (³⁄₁₆ inch thick); chill 10 minutes. Unwrap lemon dough. Roll lemon dough between sheets of plastic wrap into a 13 x 9–inch rectangle (³⁄₁₆ inch thick); chill 10 minutes. Carefully stack ginger dough on top of lemon dough, leaving a ½-inch border along one long edge. Starting with the long side without a border, roll up dough, jelly-roll fashion. Seal edge (do not seal ends of roll). Cover with plastic wrap; freeze 30 minutes.
4. Preheat oven to 350°.
5. Unwrap dough. Cut with a sharp knife into 40 slices (about ¼ inch thick). Reshape rounds, if necessary. Arrange slices 1 inch apart on baking sheets lined with parchment paper. Bake, 1 batch at a time, at 350° for 8 to 9 minutes or until set and lightly browned. Cool on wire racks. Yield: 40 cookies (serving size: 1 cookie).

CALORIES 81; **FAT** 2.8g (sat 1.7g, mono 0.7g, poly 0.2g); **PROTEIN** 1.1g; **CARB** 13.1g; **FIBER** 0.3g; **CHOL** 12mg; **IRON** 0.6mg; **SODIUM** 33mg; **CALC** 9mg

Pine Nut Cookies

Hands-on time: 30 min. Total time: 1 hr. 30 min. Pictured on page 60.

⅓ cup almond paste
¾ cup sugar
6 tablespoons butter, softened
¼ teaspoon salt
1 large egg white
½ cup pine nuts, divided
4.5 ounces all-purpose flour
(about 1 cup)
1 teaspoon baking powder

1. Preheat oven to 375°.
2. Grate almond paste on large holes of a box grater. Combine paste and next 4 ingredients (through egg white) in a large bowl; beat with a mixer at medium speed until light and fluffy (about 5 minutes).
3. Place ¼ cup pine nuts in a mini food processor; pulse until finely ground. Weigh or lightly spoon flour into a dry measuring cup; level with a knife. Combine ground nuts, flour, and baking powder, stirring with a whisk. Add flour mixture to butter mixture; beat on low speed just until combined.
4. Stack two baking sheets one on top of the other, and line the top sheet with parchment paper. Shape dough into 48 equal-sized balls (about 1 tablespoon each). Press 3 to 5 of the remaining pine nuts in a sunburst shape on top of each ball. Place 12 balls 2 inches apart on the top baking sheet (keep sheets stacked). Bake 14 minutes or until edges of cookies are lightly browned. Cool 5 minutes on pan. Cool completely on a wire rack. Repeat procedure 3 times. Yield: 24 servings (serving size: 2 cookies).

CALORIES 103; **FAT** 5.7g (sat 2g, mono 1.8g, poly 1.3g); **PROTEIN** 1.4g; **CARB** 12.2g; **FIBER** 0.4g; **CHOL** 8mg; **IRON** 0.5mg; **SODIUM** 43mg; **CALC** 22mg

QUICK TIP

Almond paste is an ingenious way to flavor, tenderize, and sweeten cookies, and it will not cause excess spreading.

NUTRITION TIP

The whole-grain cereal adds fiber, antioxidants, vitamins, and minerals. Heart-healthy, crunchy peanuts offer more fiber and minerals.

Swag Bars ◄

Hands-on time: 15 min. Total time: 15 min. These no-bake bars come together quickly with common pantry ingredients. Make sure the cereal is well crushed (try packing it in a sealed heavy-duty zip-top plastic bag and using a rolling pin) so it incorporates evenly into the peanut butter mixture.

1³/₄ cups creamy peanut butter
³/₄ cup sugar
³/₄ cup light-colored corn syrup
1¹/₂ cups (6 ounces) chopped lightly salted, dry-roasted peanuts
3¹/₂ cups (4 ounces) whole-grain flaked cereal (such as Total), finely crushed
Cooking spray
¹/₃ cup (2 ounces) chopped dark chocolate

1. Combine first 3 ingredients in a heavy saucepan over medium-high heat. Cook 4 minutes or just until mixture begins to boil, stirring constantly. Remove from heat; stir in peanuts and cereal. Spread mixture evenly into a 13 x 9–inch baking pan coated with cooking spray.
2. Place dark chocolate in a small microwave-safe bowl. Microwave at HIGH 1 minute or until chocolate melts, stirring every 20 seconds. Drizzle chocolate evenly over peanut mixture. Score into 36 bars while warm. Yield: 36 servings (serving size: 1 bar).

CALORIES 155; **FAT** 9.2g (sat 1.9g, mono 4.2g, poly 2.5g); **PROTEIN** 4.5g; **CARB** 16.2g; **FIBER** 1.5g; **CHOL** 0mg; **IRON** 2.3mg; **SODIUM** 121mg; **CALC** 113mg

Gingerbread Cookies ►

Hands-on time: 50 min. Total time: 1 hr. 42 min. Get a head start by baking cookies up to four days ahead and storing in an airtight container. Frost one day before serving; after frosting is set, pack cookies in airtight containers between layers of wax paper. This dough also makes fine slice-and-bake cookies: Form the dough into two (8-inch) round logs, and chill; slice the chilled logs into ¹/₈-inch rounds, and bake at 350° for 8 minutes or just until set and golden.

Cookies:
10.1 ounces all-purpose flour (about 2¹/₄ cups)

Keep the stream of icing moving with a slow, steady hand.

1 teaspoon ground ginger
1 teaspoon ground cinnamon
¹/₂ teaspoon baking powder
¹/₄ teaspoon baking soda
¹/₄ teaspoon salt
¹/₄ teaspoon ground nutmeg
¹/₂ cup packed brown sugar
¹/₂ cup butter, softened
3 tablespoons molasses
1 large egg
Cooking spray
Icing:
1 cup sifted powdered sugar
1 tablespoon water

1. To prepare cookies, weigh or lightly spoon flour into dry measuring cups; level with a knife. Combine flour, ginger, and next 5 ingredients (through nutmeg) in a bowl; stir with a whisk. Combine brown sugar, butter, and molasses in a large bowl; beat with a mixer at medium speed 2 minutes. Add egg; beat well. Add flour mixture to sugar mixture; beat at low speed until well blended. Divide dough in half (dough will be sticky). Gently press dough into a 4-inch circle on heavy-duty plastic wrap. Cover with additional plastic wrap; chill 1¹/₂ hours.
2. Preheat oven to 350°.
3. Roll each portion of dough to a ¹/₈-inch thickness on a floured work surface; cut with a 3-inch gingerbread man or woman cookie cutter to form 48 cookies. Place cookies 1 inch apart on a baking sheet coated with cooking spray. Bake at 350° for 8 minutes or until lightly browned. Remove cookies from baking sheet; cool completely on a wire rack.
4. To prepare the icing, combine sifted powdered sugar and 1 tablespoon water. Spoon the mixture into a zip-top plastic bag. Snip a small hole off the corner of the bag. Pipe icing onto the cookies as desired. Yield: 4 dozen (serving size: 2 cookies).

CALORIES 102; **FAT** 2.1g (sat 1.3g, mono 0.6g, poly 0.1g); **PROTEIN** 1.4g; **CARB** 19.4g; **FIBER** 0.4g; **CHOL** 14mg; **IRON** 0.8mg; **SODIUM** 67mg; **CALC** 18mg

Beat egg whites in a clean, dry, grease-free bowl.

Fresh Cherry Cheesecake Bars ▶

Hands-on time: 20 min. Total time: 4 hr. 5 min.
If you don't have fresh cherries, thawed and drained frozen cherries can be substituted. Plan ahead if you're going to take these to a party, because they need time to chill.

4.5 ounces all-purpose flour (about 1 cup)
3 tablespoons powdered sugar
1/8 teaspoon salt
5 tablespoons chilled butter, cut into small pieces
3 1/2 teaspoons ice water
1 1/4 cups chopped pitted fresh cherries
1 tablespoon granulated sugar
1 tablespoon water
2 teaspoons fresh lemon juice
1/2 teaspoon cornstarch
3/4 cup (6 ounces) 1/3-less-fat cream cheese
1/3 cup fat-free plain Greek yogurt
1/3 cup granulated sugar
1/2 teaspoon vanilla extract
1 large egg

1. Preheat oven to 350°.
2. Line an 8-inch square glass or ceramic baking dish with parchment paper. Weigh or lightly spoon flour into a dry measuring cup; level with a knife. Place flour, powdered sugar, and salt in a food processor; pulse 2 times to combine. Add chilled butter, and drizzle with ice water. Pulse 10 times or until mixture resembles coarse meal. Pour the mixture into prepared baking dish (mixture will be crumbly). Press mixture into bottom of dish. Bake at 350° for 23 minutes or until lightly browned. Cool completely. Reduce oven temperature to 325°.
3. Place cherries, 1 tablespoon granulated sugar, and 1 tablespoon water in a small saucepan. Bring to a boil. Reduce heat, and simmer 5 minutes or until cherries are tender. Combine lemon juice and cornstarch in a small bowl, stirring with a whisk. Stir cornstarch mixture into cherry mixture; cook for 1 minute or until thickened. Cool mixture slightly. Spoon the cherry mixture into food processor, and process until smooth. Spoon pureed mixture into a bowl, and set aside.
4. Wipe food processor clean. Place cream cheese and remaining ingredients in food processor; process until smooth. Spoon cream cheese mixture over cooled crust; spread evenly. Dollop cherry mixture over cream cheese mixture, and swirl together with a knife. Bake at 325° for 36 minutes or until set. Cool on a wire rack. Cover and chill at least 3 hours. Yield: 15 servings (serving size: 1 bar).

CALORIES 136; **FAT** 6.9g (sat 4g, mono 1.8g, poly 0.3g); **PROTEIN** 2.9g; **CARB** 16g; **FIBER** 0.5g; **CHOL** 33mg; **IRON** 0.5mg; **SODIUM** 92mg; **CALC** 23mg

Coconut-Almond Macaroons ◀

Look for canned almond paste alongside other baking ingredients at your market.

3 tablespoons almond paste
1 teaspoon vanilla extract
4 large egg whites, divided
1 1/3 cups powdered sugar
1 1/4 teaspoons baking powder
1/4 teaspoon salt
3 1/2 cups flaked sweetened coconut
1/2 cup granulated sugar

1. Preheat oven to 350°.
2. Combine almond paste, vanilla, and 2 egg whites in a large bowl; beat with a mixer until well blended. Combine powdered sugar, baking powder, and salt. Add powdered sugar mixture to almond paste mixture, beating until blended. Stir in coconut.
3. Place remaining 2 egg whites in a medium bowl; beat with a mixer at high speed until soft peaks form using clean, dry beaters. Gradually add granulated sugar, 1 tablespoon at a time, beating until stiff peaks form. Gently fold egg white mixture into coconut mixture.
4. Drop dough by level tablespoons 2 inches apart onto baking sheets lined with parchment paper. Bake at 350° for 17 minutes or until firm. Cool on pans 2 to 3 minutes on a wire rack. Remove cookies from pan, and cool completely on wire rack. Yield: 32 macaroons (serving size: 1 macaroon).

CALORIES 74; **FAT** 2.7g (sat 2.2g, mono 0.4g, poly 0.1g); **PROTEIN** 0.8g; **CARB** 12.2g; **FIBER** 0.9g; **CHOL** 0mg; **IRON** 0.2mg; **SODIUM** 67mg; **CALC** 14mg

These shortbread-crusted cheesecake bars
have the flavor of sweet cherries.

Mexican caramel-like dulce de leche inspired the sweet, rich icing for these chile-spiced cookies.

Mexican Spiced Shortbread Cookies ◄

Hands-on time: 50 min. Total time: 1 hr. 50 min.

Cookies:
6.75 ounces all-purpose flour (about 1½ cups)
⅓ cup unsweetened cocoa
¼ teaspoon ground cinnamon
¼ teaspoon salt
⅛ teaspoon chipotle chile powder
⅛ teaspoon ancho chile powder
½ cup unsalted butter, softened
½ cup canola oil
¾ cup powdered sugar
Icing:
2 tablespoons unsalted butter
½ cup packed light brown sugar
½ cup 1% low-fat milk
1¼ cups powdered sugar
1 teaspoon vanilla extract
Nuts:
1 teaspoon light brown sugar
1 teaspoon sea salt
1 teaspoon unsalted butter, softened
36 small pecan halves

1. Preheat oven to 325°.
2. To prepare cookies, weigh or lightly spoon flour into dry measuring cups; level with a knife. Combine flour, cocoa, and next 4 ingredients (through ancho chile powder) in a bowl; stir with a whisk.
3. Place ½ cup butter in a large bowl; beat with a mixer at medium speed until light and fluffy. Gradually add oil; beat 3 minutes or until well blended. Gradually add ¾ cup powdered sugar; beat well. Add flour mixture; beat at low speed until well blended. Cover and chill 30 minutes.
4. Shape dough into 36 balls. Place 2 inches apart on an ungreased baking sheet. Flatten cookies to ¼ inch thickness. Bake at 325° for 20 minutes. Cool 1 minute on baking sheet. Remove from baking sheet to a wire rack; cool completely.

➤ FLAVOR HIT

Make a double batch of the sugared pecans. Serve over ice cream, or toss with salads to add a sweet crunch.

5. To prepare icing, melt 2 tablespoons butter in a large saucepan over medium heat. Add ½ cup brown sugar and milk; cook 1 minute or until sugar dissolves, stirring constantly. Bring to a boil; reduce heat, and simmer 3 minutes or until slightly thickened, stirring occasionally. Remove from heat; cool to room temperature. Add powdered sugar and vanilla, stirring with a whisk until smooth.
6. To prepare nuts, combine 1 teaspoon brown sugar, sea salt, and 1 teaspoon butter in a medium bowl. Arrange pecans on a baking sheet. Bake at 325° for 10 minutes or until toasted. Add hot pecans to butter mixture, tossing well to coat. Cool.
7. Spread 1 teaspoon icing over each cookie; top each with 1 pecan half. Yield: 3 dozen (serving size: 1 cookie).

CALORIES 125; **FAT** 7.5g (sat 2.4g, mono 3.3g, poly 1.4g); **PROTEIN** 1g; **CARB** 14.5g; **FIBER** 0.6g; **CHOL** 9mg; **IRON** 0.5mg; **SODIUM** 85mg; **CALC** 11mg

Toasted Coconut Chocolate Chunk Cookies ▼

Hands-on time: 20 min. Total time: 40 min.
Given that both chocolate and coconut are not as "bad" as once thought, and given that they taste mighty good together, we baked up a batch of these toasty, chocolaty treats to celebrate. Like all sweets with few other nutrients, though, they are treats—perfectly healthy every once in a while.

1 cup flaked sweetened coconut
4.5 ounces all-purpose flour (about 1 cup)
½ teaspoon baking powder
¼ teaspoon baking soda
⅛ teaspoon salt
¾ cup packed brown sugar
¼ cup unsalted butter, softened
1 teaspoon vanilla extract
1 large egg
2 ounces dark chocolate (70% cacao), chopped
Cooking spray

1. Preheat oven to 350°.
2. Arrange coconut in a single layer in a small baking pan. Bake at 350° for 7 minutes or until lightly toasted, stirring once. Set aside to cool.

{ fyi }

Bake cookies on heavy, shiny metal baking sheets; cookies baked on nonstick sheets tend to brown too much on the bottom. We don't advise using jelly-roll pans—the rims can deflect heat. Lining pans with parchment paper is optional but it prevents sticking.

3. Weigh or lightly spoon flour into a dry measuring cup; level with a knife. Combine flour, baking powder, baking soda, and salt in a medium bowl; stir with a whisk until blended. Place sugar and butter in a large bowl; beat with a mixer at medium speed until well blended. Beat in vanilla and egg. Add flour mixture, beating at low speed just until combined. Stir in toasted coconut and chocolate.
4. Drop by level tablespoons 2 inches apart onto baking sheets coated with cooking spray. Bake at 350° for 10 minutes or until bottoms of cookies just begin to brown. Remove from pan, and cool completely on wire racks. Yield: 25 servings (serving size: 1 cookie).

CALORIES 88; **FAT** 3.8g (sat 2.5g, mono 0.6g, poly 0.1g); **PROTEIN** 1g; **CARB** 13g; **FIBER** 0.4g; **CHOL** 12mg; **IRON** 0.6mg; **SODIUM** 38mg; **CALC** 15mg

If you prefer a fudgy filling, use chocolate chips.

Almond Butter Snickerdoodles ▶

Hands-on time: 25 min. Total time: 40 min.

1 cup packed brown sugar
¹⁄₃ cup (about 3 ounces) ¹⁄₃-less-fat cream cheese, softened
¹⁄₄ cup unsalted butter, softened
2 tablespoons smooth almond butter
1 teaspoon grated lemon rind
1 teaspoon vanilla extract
2 large egg yolks, lightly beaten
4.75 ounces white whole-wheat flour (about 1 cup)
1.5 ounces whole-wheat flour (about ¹⁄₃ cup)
1 teaspoon baking soda
1¹⁄₂ teaspoons ground cinnamon, divided
¹⁄₂ teaspoon salt
2 tablespoons granulated sugar

1. Preheat oven to 350°.
2. Line a large baking sheet with parchment paper.
3. Place first 4 ingredients in a medium bowl, and beat with a mixer at high speed until well combined (about 2 minutes). Add 1 teaspoon lemon rind, vanilla extract, and egg yolks; beat until well blended.
4. Weigh or lightly spoon flours into dry measuring cups; level with a knife. Combine flours, baking soda, ¹⁄₂ teaspoon ground cinnamon, and ¹⁄₂ teaspoon salt; stir with a whisk. Add flour mixture to butter mixture; beat at low speed until well combined. Drop half of the dough by rounded tablespoons onto prepared baking sheet. Combine remaining 1 teaspoon cinnamon and granulated sugar in a small bowl, and sprinkle half of the cinnamon-sugar mixture evenly over cookies. Bake at 350° for 6 minutes; flatten cookies with the back of a spatula. Bake an additional 6 minutes. Cool on pans 1 minute. Remove from pans, and cool on wire racks. Repeat procedure with remaining dough and sugar mixture. Yield: 2 dozen (serving size: 1 cookie).

Butterscotch Bars ▲

Hands-on time: 20 min. Total time: 50 min.
A small square of these rich bars is enough to satisfy a dessert craving. The flour-and-oats mixture is somewhat dry after combining, but it serves as both a solid base for the soft butterscotch chip layer and a crumbly, streusel-like topping.

1 cup packed brown sugar
5 tablespoons butter, melted
1 teaspoon vanilla extract
1 large egg, lightly beaten
9 ounces all-purpose flour (about 2 cups)
2¹⁄₂ cups quick-cooking oats
¹⁄₂ teaspoon salt
¹⁄₂ teaspoon baking soda
Cooking spray
³⁄₄ cup fat-free sweetened condensed milk
1¹⁄₄ cups butterscotch morsels (about 8 ounces)
¹⁄₈ teaspoon salt
¹⁄₂ cup finely chopped walnuts, toasted

1. Preheat oven to 350°.
2. Combine sugar and butter in a large bowl. Stir in vanilla and egg. Weigh or lightly spoon flour into dry measuring cups; level with a knife. Combine flour, oats, ¹⁄₂ teaspoon salt, and baking soda in a bowl. Add oat mixture to sugar mixture; stir with a fork until combined (mixture will be crumbly). Place 3 cups oat mixture into the bottom of a 13 x 9–inch metal baking pan coated with cooking spray; press into bottom of pan. Set aside.
3. Place sweetened condensed milk, butterscotch morsels, and ¹⁄₈ teaspoon salt in a microwave-safe bowl; microwave at HIGH 1 minute or until butterscotch morsels melt, stirring every 20 seconds. Stir in walnuts. Scrape mixture into pan, spreading evenly over crust. Sprinkle evenly with remaining oat mixture, gently pressing into butterscotch mixture. Bake at 350° for 30 minutes or until the topping is golden brown. Place pan on a cooling rack; run a knife around outside edge. Cool completely. Yield: 36 servings (serving size: 1 bar).

CALORIES 148; **FAT** 5.1g (sat 2.7g, mono 0.9g, poly 1.1g); **PROTEIN** 2.6g; **CARB** 23.4g; **FIBER** 0.8g; **CHOL** 11mg; **IRON** 0.8mg; **SODIUM** 87mg; **CALC** 31mg

CALORIES 104; **FAT** 3.8g (sat 1.9g, mono 1.2g, poly 0.3g); **PROTEIN** 1.6g; **CARB** 16.2g; **FIBER** 0.5g; **CHOL** 25mg; **IRON** 0.7mg; **SODIUM** 127mg; **CALC** 19mg

Almond butter
is mildly sweet
and lends a
roasted almond
taste.

PREP POINTER

Bake these brownies in shiny metal pans, not glass or ceramic dishes. Glass conducts heat differently and can bake the brownies too quickly.

Black and Tan Brownies ◄

Hands-on time: 30 min. Total time: 1 hr. 10 min.
Historically, the phrase "black and tan" referred to the much-reviled auxiliary force of English soldiers sent to Ireland to suppress the Irish rebels after the 1916 Easter Rising. Eventually, a much-loved drink made with half Guinness Stout and half Harp Lager assumed the name, and now this two-toned brownie (with the addition of Guinness) shares it.

Tan brownies:
6 tablespoons butter, softened
1¹/₂ cups packed brown sugar
2 large eggs
1 teaspoon vanilla extract
4.5 ounces all-purpose flour
(about 1 cup)
1 teaspoon baking powder
¹/₄ teaspoon salt
¹/₂ cup chopped pecans
Cooking spray
Black brownies:
3 ounces unsweetened chocolate, finely chopped
4 tablespoons butter
1 cup granulated sugar
2 large eggs
1 teaspoon vanilla extract
1 cup Guinness Stout
4.5 ounces all-purpose flour
(about 1 cup)
¹/₄ teaspoon salt

1. Place one rack in lower third of oven; place another rack in center of oven. Preheat oven to 350°.
2. To prepare tan brownies, place 6 tablespoons butter and brown sugar in a medium bowl; beat with a mixer at medium speed until light and fluffy. Beat in 2 eggs and 1 teaspoon vanilla. Weigh or lightly spoon 4.5 ounces (about 1 cup) flour into a dry measuring cup; level with a knife. Combine 4.5 ounces flour, baking powder, and ¹/₄ teaspoon salt, stirring well. Add flour mixture and pecans to sugar mixture, beating just until combined. Spoon into a 13 x 9–inch metal baking pan coated with cooking spray, spreading evenly with a knife or rubber spatula. Bake at 350° in lower third of oven for 15 minutes.
3. To prepare black brownies, place chocolate and 4 tablespoons butter in

a large microwave-safe bowl; microwave at HIGH for 1 minute or until melted, stirring every 20 seconds until smooth. Add granulated sugar, stirring until well combined. Add 2 eggs, 1 teaspoon vanilla, and Guinness, stirring with a whisk until well combined. Weigh or lightly spoon 4.5 ounces (about 1 cup) flour into a dry measuring cup; level with a knife. Combine 4.5 ounces flour and ¹/₄ teaspoon salt, stirring well. Add flour mixture to chocolate mixture, stirring to combine. Pour mixture evenly over tan brownies.
4. Bake on the center rack at 350° for 25 minutes or until a wooden pick inserted into center comes out almost clean. Cool in pan on a wire rack; cut into squares. Yield: 32 squares (serving size: 1 square).

CALORIES 162; **FAT** 7g (sat 3.4g, mono 2.4g, poly 0.7g); **PROTEIN** 2.2g; **CARB** 23.7g; **FIBER** 0.8g; **CHOL** 36mg; **IRON** 1.2mg; **SODIUM** 87mg; **CALC** 29mg

{ fyi }

For twice-baked cookies like biscotti, leave plenty of space between the dough rolls so they don't spread and bake together. After the first bake, they will be crunchy. Use a serrated knife to slice without crumbling.

Deep Dark Chocolate Biscotti ◄

Hands-on time: 20 min. Total time: 1 hr. 12 min.

9.5 ounces whole-wheat flour (about 2 cups)
2 tablespoons flaxseed
¹/₂ teaspoon baking soda
¹/₄ teaspoon salt
¹/₃ cup granulated sugar
¹/₃ cup packed dark brown sugar
2 large egg whites
1 large egg
1¹/₂ teaspoons vanilla extract
²/₃ cup dark chocolate chips (such as Hershey's)
³/₄ cup unsalted almonds

1. Preheat oven to 350°.
2. Weigh or lightly spoon flour into dry measuring cups; level with a knife. Combine flour, flaxseed, soda, and salt in a bowl, stirring with a whisk. Combine sugars, egg whites, and egg in a bowl; beat with a mixer at high speed for 2 minutes. Add vanilla; mix well. Add flour mixture to egg mixture; stir until combined. Fold in chocolate and almonds. Divide dough into 3 equal portions. Roll each portion into a 6-inch-long roll. Arrange rolls 3 inches apart on a baking sheet lined with parchment paper. Pat to a 1-inch thickness. Bake at 350° for 28 minutes or until firm.
3. Remove rolls from baking sheet; cool 10 minutes on a wire rack. Cut rolls diagonally into 30 (¹/₂-inch) slices. Place, cut sides down, on baking sheet. Reduce oven temperature to 325°; bake 7 minutes. Turn cookies over; bake 7 minutes (cookies will be slightly soft in center but will harden as they cool). Remove from baking sheet; cool on wire rack. Yield: 2¹/₂ dozen (serving size: 1 biscotto).

CALORIES 94; **FAT** 3.5g (sat 0.9g, mono 1.7g, poly 0.7g); **PROTEIN** 2.7g; **CARB** 14.4g; **FIBER** 1.9g; **CHOL** 7mg; **IRON** 0.7mg; **SODIUM** 49mg; **CALC** 18mg

 NUTRITION TIP
Whole-wheat flour, flaxseed, and unsalted almonds add fiber and antioxidants to these cookies.

Fudgy Brownies ▼
Hands-on time: 15 min. Total time: 35 min.

4.5 ounces all-purpose flour (1 cup)
1/2 cup unsweetened cocoa
1/4 teaspoon salt
1/3 cup butter
2 ounces dark chocolate, chopped
1 cup granulated sugar
1/4 cup 1% low-fat milk
1 teaspoon vanilla extract
2 large egg yolks
1 large egg
Cooking spray

1. Preheat oven to 350°.
2. Weigh or lightly spoon flour into a dry measuring cup; level with a knife. Combine flour, cocoa, and salt in a medium bowl; stir with a whisk.
3. Place butter and chocolate in a medium microwave-safe bowl, and microwave at HIGH for 45 seconds, stirring every 15 seconds. Stir until smooth, and set aside. Cool slightly. Add 1 cup sugar, milk, 1 teaspoon vanilla extract, egg yolks, and egg; stir with a whisk to combine. Add butter mixture to flour mixture, stirring just until combined. Pour batter into an 8-inch square metal baking pan coated with cooking spray. Bake at 350° for 20 minutes or until a wooden pick inserted in center comes out almost clean. Yield: 16 squares (serving size: 1 square).

CALORIES 147; FAT 6.1g (sat 3.6g, mono 1.5g, poly 0.3g); PROTEIN 2.3g; CARB 22.4g; FIBER 1.3g; CHOL 47mg; IRON 1mg; SODIUM 73mg; CALC 15mg

Banana-Oatmeal Chocolate Chip Cookies ▶
Hands-on time: 18 min. Total time: 35 min.

1/2 cup mashed ripe banana (about 1 medium)
1/2 cup packed brown sugar
1/4 cup butter, softened
1/4 cup granulated sugar
1 teaspoon vanilla extract
1 large egg
5.6 ounces all-purpose flour (about 1 1/4 cups)
2 cups old-fashioned oats
1 teaspoon baking soda
1/2 teaspoon salt
1/2 cup semisweet chocolate chips
Cooking spray

1. Preheat oven to 350°.
2. Combine first 5 ingredients in a large bowl; beat with a mixer at medium speed until smooth. Add egg; beat well.

{ fyi }

Always place the mounds of dough on cool baking sheets— warm or hot pans will cause the cookies to spread or puff too much. You can quickly cool the baking sheet under cold water, and dry thoroughly before using it for the next batch.

3. Weigh or lightly spoon flour into dry measuring cups; level with a knife. Combine flour, oats, baking soda, and salt in a medium bowl, stirring with a whisk. Add flour mixture to banana mixture in bowl; beat with a mixer at medium speed until well blended. Stir in chocolate chips.
4. Drop batter by heaping tablespoonfuls 2 inches apart onto baking sheets coated with cooking spray. Bake at 350° for 18 minutes or until golden. Cool on pans 2 minutes. Remove cookies from pans; cool completely on wire racks. Yield: 2 dozen (serving size: 1 cookie).

CALORIES 115; FAT 3.6g (sat 2g, mono 1.1g, poly 0.3g); PROTEIN 2g; CARB 19.1g; FIBER 1.2g; CHOL 14mg; IRON 0.9mg; SODIUM 121mg; CALC 10mg

Check a minute or two early to avoid overbaking.

Black Forest
Cherry Cake,
page 78

cakes & cupcakes

From one-pan wonders to multitiered affairs, these light and tender goodies let you wow your crowd with the ultimate bakery treat.

Lemon-Rosemary Olive Oil Cake ▶

Hands-on time: 25 min. Total time: 1 hr. 25 min.
Fresh rosemary lends evergreen essence, while olive oil enhances the flavor and maintains the moist texture of this Mediterranean-inspired cake.

Cooking spray
2 tablespoons all-purpose flour
13.5 ounces all-purpose flour (about 3 cups)
1½ tablespoons finely chopped fresh rosemary
2 teaspoons baking powder
½ teaspoon baking soda
½ teaspoon salt
1½ cups granulated sugar
½ cup olive oil
½ cup fat-free milk
2 teaspoons grated lemon rind
¼ cup fresh lemon juice
½ teaspoon vanilla extract
¼ teaspoon lemon extract
3 large eggs
1 cup powdered sugar
1 tablespoon fresh lemon juice

1. Preheat oven to 350°.
2. Coat a 10-inch tube pan with cooking spray; dust with 2 tablespoons flour. Weigh or lightly spoon 13.5 ounces flour (about 3 cups) into dry measuring cups; level with a knife. Combine flour and next 4 ingredients (through salt) in a large bowl.
3. Place granulated sugar and next 7 ingredients (through eggs) in a medium bowl; beat with a mixer at low speed 2 minutes or until smooth. Add to flour mixture; beat until blended.
4. Pour batter into prepared pan. Bake at 350° for 45 minutes or until a wooden pick inserted in center comes out clean. Cool in pan for 15 minutes on a wire rack, and remove from pan. Cool completely on wire rack. Combine powdered sugar and 1 tablespoon lemon juice, stirring until smooth. Drizzle sugar mixture over cake.
Yield: 16 servings (serving size: 1 slice).

CALORIES 265; FAT 7.9g (sat 1.3g, mono 5.3g, poly 0.9g); PROTEIN 3.9g; CARB 45.1g; FIBER 0.7g; CHOL 40mg; IRON 1.3mg; SODIUM 211mg; CALC 20mg

{ fyi }

Because precision is crucial with light baked goods, follow these important steps to ensure success: Preheat the oven; weigh or measure flour properly; and use the ingredients, especially flour, in the amounts specified in the recipe.

Black Forest Cherry Cake

Hands-on time: 40 min. Total time: 1 hr. 25 min. The heavy cherry filling may cause the cake, shown on page 76, to sink slightly in the center once assembled, but it won't detract from the stunning presentation, which is easier to prepare than it appears. Canned or jarred Montmorency cherries in water have a more vibrant crimson color than most varieties you find in local supermarkets. It's worth the time to check out specialty grocery stores or to order them online (try kingorchards.com) for this impressive dessert.

Filling:
⅔ cup sugar
⅔ cup cranberry juice cocktail
¼ cup water
3 tablespoons cornstarch
2 (14.5-ounce) cans pitted tart cherries in water, drained
Cake:
7.75 ounces all-purpose flour (about 1¾ cups)
2 cups sugar
¾ cup unsweetened cocoa
2 teaspoons baking soda
1 teaspoon baking powder
¼ teaspoon salt
1 cup nonfat buttermilk
1 cup fat-free milk
¼ cup canola oil
1 teaspoon vanilla extract
2 large eggs
Cooking spray
2 cups frozen reduced-fat whipped topping, thawed
1 tablespoon kirsch (cherry brandy)
½ ounce dark chocolate curls

1. To prepare filling, combine first 4 ingredients in a large saucepan; stir until cornstarch dissolves. Heat pan over medium-high heat; bring to a boil, stirring constantly. Cook 1 minute or until sugar mixture is very thick, stirring constantly. Remove sugar mixture from heat. Stir in cherries. Cool completely; cover and set aside.
2. To prepare cake, preheat the oven to 350°.
3. Weigh or lightly spoon flour into dry measuring cups; level with a knife. Combine flour and next 5 ingredients (through salt) in a large bowl; stir with a whisk. Combine buttermilk, milk, oil, vanilla, and eggs in a bowl; stir with a whisk. Add buttermilk mixture to sugar mixture; beat with a mixer at medium speed just until well blended (batter will be thin).
4. Pour batter into 2 (9-inch) round cake pans coated with cooking spray. Bake at 350° for 40 minutes or until a wooden pick inserted in center comes out clean. Cool in pans 10 minutes; remove from pans. Cool completely on a wire rack.
5. Place 1 cake layer on a plate, and spoon half of cherry mixture (about 1½ cups) evenly over the top, leaving a ¼-inch border around edges. Combine whipped topping and kirsch in a small bowl. Spoon 1 cup whipped topping mixture evenly over cherry mixture. Top with remaining cake layer. Spoon remaining 1½ cups cherry mixture onto cake layer, leaving a ½-inch border around edges. Spoon remaining 1 cup whipped topping mixture onto cherry mixture, leaving a 2-inch border from the edge of the cake layer. Garnish with chocolate curls. Cover loosely, and chill until ready to serve.
Yield: 16 servings (serving size: 1 piece).

CALORIES 295; FAT 6.4g (sat 2.3g, mono 2.5g, poly 1.2g); PROTEIN 4.4g; CARB 58.2g; FIBER 2.1g; CHOL 27mg; IRON 1.9mg; SODIUM 259mg; CALC 70mg

SIMPLE SWAP

If you want a nonalcoholic substitute or don't have kirsch, try the juice of maraschino cherries.

Apple Upside-Down Cake ◄

Hands-on time: 35 min. Total time: 1 hr. 15 min. Mild Rome apples are great for baking. You can also use Pink Lady, Honeycrisp, or Jonagold apples. Dollop the cake with a bit of whipped cream, if desired.

Topping:
Cooking spray
¾ cup sugar
¼ cup water
3 cups (¼-inch-thick) slices peeled Rome apples (about 2 large)
¼ cup chopped walnuts
Cake:
5.3 ounces cake flour (about 1⅓ cups)
1½ teaspoons baking powder
¼ teaspoon salt
⅔ cup sugar
3 tablespoons butter, softened
2 large egg yolks
1 teaspoon vanilla extract
½ cup 1% low-fat milk
3 large egg whites

1. Preheat oven to 350°. Coat a 9-inch round cake pan with cooking spray.
2. To prepare topping, combine ¾ cup sugar and ¼ cup water in a small heavy saucepan over medium-high heat; cook until sugar dissolves, stirring gently as needed to dissolve sugar evenly (about 3 minutes). Continue cooking for 4 minutes or until golden (do not stir). Immediately pour into prepared cake pan, tipping quickly to coat bottom of pan. Arrange apple slices in concentric circles in pan over the warm caramel. Sprinkle with nuts; set aside.
3. To prepare cake, weigh or lightly spoon flour into dry measuring cups, and level with a knife. Combine flour, baking powder, and salt, and stir with a whisk.
4. Combine ⅔ cup sugar and butter in a large bowl; beat with a mixer at medium speed until light and fluffy. Add egg yolks and vanilla to sugar mixture; beat until combined. Add flour mixture and milk alternately to sugar mixture, beginning and ending with flour mixture; mix after each addition.
5. Place egg whites in a large, clean bowl. Beat egg whites with mixer at high speed until stiff peaks form using clean, dry beaters. Gently fold egg whites into batter. Spread batter over apples. Bake at 350° for 35 minutes or until a wooden pick inserted in center comes out clean. Cool on a wire rack in pan for 5 minutes. Loosen edges of cake with a knife; invert cake onto a serving plate. Serve warm or at room temperature. Yield: 10 servings (serving size: 1 slice).

CALORIES 253; **FAT** 6.6g (sat 2.8g, mono 1.6g, poly 1.7g); **PROTEIN** 3.9g; **CARB** 45.8g; **FIBER** 0.9g; **CHOL** 52mg; **IRON** 1.5mg; **SODIUM** 163mg; **CALC** 79mg

Carrot Cake ▼

Hands-on time: 35 min. Total time: 1 hr. 53 min. Warm spices and brown sugar add rich, caramelized flavors to this carrot cake. If you can't find fromage blanc, use more cream cheese.

Cake:
10.1 ounces all-purpose flour (about 2¼ cups)
2 teaspoons baking powder
1½ teaspoons ground cinnamon
¼ teaspoon salt
2 cups grated carrot
1 cup granulated sugar
½ cup packed brown sugar
6 tablespoons butter, softened
3 large eggs
1 teaspoon vanilla extract
½ cup low-fat buttermilk
Cooking spray
Frosting:
6 ounces cream cheese, softened
1 ounce fromage blanc
2 tablespoons butter, softened
½ teaspoon vanilla extract
⅛ teaspoon salt
3 cups powdered sugar
¼ cup chopped pecans, toasted

1. Preheat oven to 350°.
2. To prepare cake, weigh or lightly spoon flour into dry measuring cups, and level with a knife. Combine flour, 2 teaspoons baking powder, ground cinnamon, and ¼ teaspoon salt in a medium bowl, stirring with a whisk. Add 2 cups grated carrot, and toss to combine.
3. Place granulated sugar, brown sugar, and 6 tablespoons butter in a large bowl. Beat with a mixer at medium speed until combined. Add eggs, 1 at a time, beating well after each addition. Stir in 1 teaspoon vanilla. Add flour mixture and buttermilk alternately to sugar mixture, beginning and ending with flour mixture. Spread batter into a 13 x 9–inch metal baking pan coated with cooking spray. Bake at 350° for 28 minutes or until a wooden pick inserted in center comes out clean. Cool cake completely on a wire rack.
4. To prepare frosting, place softened cream cheese and next 4 ingredients (through ⅛ teaspoon salt) in a medium bowl. Beat with a mixer at medium speed until fluffy. Gradually add powdered sugar, beating at medium speed until combined (don't overbeat). Spread frosting evenly over top of cake. Sprinkle evenly with toasted pecans. Yield: 20 servings (serving size: 1 piece).

CALORIES 284; **FAT** 9.7g (sat 4.9g, mono 2.8g, poly 0.8g); **PROTEIN** 3.6g; **CARB** 46.6g; **FIBER** 0.9g; **CHOL** 49mg; **IRON** 1mg; **SODIUM** 172mg; **CALC** 68mg

Ours is 900 calories less than an over-the-top recipe.

Prepare the compote while the cake is in the oven.

Tuscan Cake with Citrus Compote ▲

Hands-on time: 35 min. Total time: 1 hr. 35 min.

Cake:
1/2 cup sugar
6 tablespoons extra-virgin olive oil
2 large eggs
1 tablespoon grated grapefruit rind
1 1/2 teaspoons grated lime rind
1/2 teaspoon vanilla extract
1 (6-ounce) container plain low-fat yogurt
5.6 ounces all-purpose flour (about 1 1/4 cups)
1.5 ounces fine yellow cornmeal (about 1/4 cup)
3/4 teaspoon baking soda
1/4 teaspoon baking powder
1/4 teaspoon salt
Cooking spray
Compote:
2 large red grapefruit
4 large oranges
2 tablespoons fresh lime juice
3 tablespoons honey
1/8 teaspoon ground allspice

1. Preheat oven to 325°.
2. To prepare cake, place sugar and oil in a large bowl; beat with a mixer at high speed for 2 minutes or until well blended. Add eggs, 1 at a time, beating well after each addition. Add rinds, vanilla extract, and yogurt; beat until combined.
3. Weigh or lightly spoon flour and cornmeal into dry measuring cups; level with a knife. Combine flour, cornmeal, baking soda, baking powder, and salt, stirring with a whisk. Add flour mixture to oil mixture; stir with a whisk just until combined. Pour batter into a 9-inch springform pan coated with cooking spray. Bake at 325° for 30 minutes or until golden brown and a wooden pick inserted in center comes out clean. Cool 10 minutes on a wire rack; remove sides from pan. Cool cake completely on rack.
4. To prepare compote, peel and section grapefruit and oranges over a medium bowl, reserving juices; place sections in another bowl. Combine reserved juices and lime juice in a small saucepan; bring to a boil. Stir in honey and allspice; reduce heat, and simmer 4 minutes or until syrupy. Cover and chill 30 minutes. Pour over fruit sections; toss gently. Chill. Serve compote over cake. Yield: 9 servings (serving size: 1 cake wedge and about 1/4 cup compote).

CALORIES 305; FAT 10.7g (sat 1.8g, mono 7.1g, poly 1.2g); PROTEIN 5.4g; CARB 48.9g; FIBER 2.8g; CHOL 48mg; IRON 1.4mg; SODIUM 211mg; CALC 88mg

Clementine-Date Cake ▶

Hands-on time: 30 min. Total time: 1 hr. 15 min.

Cooking spray
2 teaspoons all-purpose flour
1/2 cup walnut halves, divided
6 pitted dates
2 unpeeled clementines, quartered
1/2 cup packed brown sugar
3 tablespoons unsalted butter, softened
2 tablespoons toasted walnut oil
3/4 teaspoon vanilla extract
1 large egg
9 ounces all-purpose flour (2 cups)
3/4 teaspoon baking soda
3/8 teaspoon salt
1/2 cup fat-free buttermilk
1/3 cup chopped pitted dates
1 cup powdered sugar
5 teaspoons fresh tangerine juice

1. Preheat oven to 350°.
2. Coat a 9-inch round cake pan with cooking spray. Line bottom of pan with parchment paper; coat with cooking spray. Dust with 2 teaspoons flour.
3. Reserve 5 walnuts. Place remaining nuts, 6 dates, and clementines in food processor; process until ground.
4. Combine brown sugar, butter, and oil; beat with a mixer at medium speed until blended. Beat in vanilla and egg.
5. Weigh or lightly spoon flour into dry measuring cups; level with a knife. Combine flour, baking soda, and salt. Add flour mixture and buttermilk alternately to sugar mixture, beginning and ending with flour mixture; mix after each addition. Add nut mixture and chopped dates; beat at medium speed 3 minutes. Pour batter into prepared pan. Bake at 350° for 45 minutes or until a wooden pick inserted in center comes out clean. Cool in pan 10 minutes on a wire rack; remove from pan.
6. Whisk powdered sugar and juice in small bowl until smooth. Drizzle glaze over warm cake; spread to coat top. Top with reserved 5 walnuts. Cool on a wire rack 30 minutes. Yield: 12 servings (serving size: 1 slice).

CALORIES 266; FAT 8.5g (sat 2.5g, mono 1.8g, poly 3.7g); PROTEIN 4.1g; CARB 44.8g; FIBER 1.7g; CHOL 25mg; IRON 1.4mg; SODIUM 172mg; CALC 39mg

FLAVOR HIT
This moist, dense cake includes two entire clementines—not only the juice and flesh, but also the skin, which is filled with aromatic oils.

This pudding-like date cake
is smothered in a rich coconut
and brown sugar topping.

Sticky Date and Coconut Cake ◄

Hands-on time: 27 min. Total time: 1 hr.

Cake:
1 cup chopped pitted dates
1 cup water
1 teaspoon baking soda
3 tablespoons butter
Dash of salt
6.75 ounces all-purpose flour
    (about 1½ cups)
1 teaspoon baking powder
½ teaspoon salt
1 cup granulated sugar
1 teaspoon vanilla extract
1 large egg, lightly beaten
Cooking spray
Topping:
⅔ cup packed light brown sugar
½ cup flaked sweetened coconut
2½ tablespoons butter
2 teaspoons fat-free milk

1. Preheat oven to 350°.
2. To prepare cake, combine first 5 ingredients in a small saucepan; bring to a boil, stirring occasionally. Remove from heat, and let stand 10 minutes or until dates are tender.
3. Weigh or lightly spoon flour into dry measuring cups; level with a knife. Combine flour, baking powder, and ½ teaspoon salt in a bowl. Stir in date mixture, granulated sugar, vanilla, and egg until well combined. Pour batter into a 9-inch springform pan coated with cooking spray. Bake at 350° for 20 minutes. Remove cake from oven.
4. To prepare topping, combine brown sugar and the remaining ingredients in a small saucepan; bring to a boil. Reduce heat, and simmer for 1 minute. Pour brown sugar mixture over cake; bake at 350° for an additional 13 minutes or until a wooden pick inserted in center comes out clean. Cool in pan 5 minutes on a wire rack. Run a knife around outside edge. Cool completely on a wire rack. Yield: 12 servings (serving size: 1 wedge).

CALORIES 268; **FAT** 6.5g (sat 4.2g, mono 1.6g, poly 0.3g); **PROTEIN** 2.5g; **CARB** 51.6g; **FIBER** 1.7g; **CHOL** 31mg; **IRON** 1.2mg; **SODIUM** 313mg; **CALC** 46mg

Salted Chocolate Ganache Cake ▼

Hands-on time: 25 min. Total time: 1 hr. Choose a premium chocolate bar for this simple one-layer cake. Make up to one day ahead, and store in an airtight container.

Cooking spray
2 teaspoons cake flour
5.3 ounces sifted cake flour
    (about 1¼ cups)
1½ teaspoons baking powder
½ cup packed dark brown sugar
¼ cup butter, softened
1 large egg
¾ cup evaporated fat-free milk
1 teaspoon vanilla extract
2 large egg whites
3 tablespoons dark brown sugar
2½ ounces dark chocolate,
    divided
1 tablespoon butter
¼ teaspoon sea salt or fleur de sel

1. Preheat oven to 350°.
2. Coat 1 (9-inch) round cake pan with cooking spray; dust with 2 teaspoons flour.
3. Weigh or lightly spoon 5.3 ounces flour into dry measuring cups; level with a knife. Combine flour and baking powder in a bowl; stir with a whisk. Place ½ cup sugar and ¼ cup butter in a large bowl; beat with a mixer at medium speed until well blended (about 5 minutes). Add egg; mix well. Add flour mixture to sugar mixture alternately with milk, beginning and ending with flour mixture. Stir in vanilla.
4. Beat egg whites with a mixer at high speed until foamy using clean, dry beaters. Gradually add 3 tablespoons sugar, beating until stiff peaks form. Gently fold half of egg white mixture into flour mixture; fold in remaining egg white mixture. Grate ½ ounce chocolate; fold grated chocolate into batter. Pour batter into prepared pan. Bake at 350° for 23 minutes or until a wooden pick inserted near center comes out clean. Cool in pan 10 minutes. Remove from pan; cool completely on a wire rack.
5. Chop remaining 2 ounces chocolate. Combine chopped chocolate and 1 tablespoon butter in a microwave-safe bowl. Microwave at MEDIUM 1 minute or until chocolate melts, stirring every 15 seconds. Spread chocolate mixture over top of cake; sprinkle evenly with sea salt. Cut into 8 wedges. Yield: 8 servings (serving size: 1 wedge).

CALORIES 263; **FAT** 10.9g (sat 6.4g, mono 2.1g, poly 0.4g); **PROTEIN** 5.3g; **CARB** 37.6g; **FIBER** 0.7g; **CHOL** 47mg; **IRON** 2.2mg; **SODIUM** 248mg; **CALC** 156mg

Pear-Walnut Cake with Honey-Orange Syrup ▶

Hands-on time: 25 min. Total time: 1 hr. 35 min. Brushing the honey-orange syrup over the warm cake infuses it with moisture and delicate aromas. For a second-day treat, try toasting a leftover slice.

Cake:
Cooking spray
2 tablespoons all-purpose flour
1³⁄₄ cups sugar
4 large eggs
13.5 ounces all-purpose flour
  (about 3 cups)
1 tablespoon baking powder
1 teaspoon aniseed, crushed
¹⁄₂ teaspoon kosher salt
¹⁄₂ teaspoon ground cinnamon
1 teaspoon finely grated orange rind
¹⁄₂ cup fresh orange juice
¹⁄₂ cup canola oil
1 teaspoon vanilla extract
2 cups chopped peeled pear (about 3)
¹⁄₄ cup chopped walnuts, toasted
Syrup:
¹⁄₃ cup honey
2 tablespoons fresh orange juice

1. Preheat oven to 375°.
2. To prepare cake, coat a 10-inch tube pan with cooking spray; dust with 2 tablespoons flour. Set aside.
3. Place 1¹⁄₄ cups sugar and eggs in a large bowl; beat with a mixer at medium speed until thick and pale (about 3 minutes).
4. Weigh or lightly spoon 3 cups flour into dry measuring cups; level with a knife. Combine flour, baking powder, aniseed, salt, and cinnamon, stirring well with a whisk.
5. Combine grated orange rind, ¹⁄₂ cup orange juice, canola oil, and vanilla. Add flour mixture to egg mixture alternately with juice mixture, beginning and ending with flour mixture; blend after each addition just until combined. Stir in pear and walnuts. Pour batter into prepared pan. Bake at 375° for 55 minutes or until a wooden pick inserted in center comes out clean. Cool in pan on a wire rack 15 minutes; loosen cake from sides of pan using a narrow metal spatula or knife. Remove cake from pan.

6. To prepare syrup, combine honey and 2 tablespoons juice in a small saucepan over medium heat. Cook 2 minutes, stirring constantly. Brush warm syrup over top and sides of cake. Cool completely. Yield: 18 servings (serving size: 1 slice).

CALORIES 271; FAT 8.9g (sat 0.9g, mono 4.3g, poly 2.9g); PROTEIN 4.1g; CARB 45.4g; FIBER 1.4g; CHOL 47mg; IRON 1.4mg; SODIUM 176mg; CALC 15mg

Pecan Spice Cake with Maple Frosting ▶

Hands-on time: 40 min. Total time: 1 hr. 30 min. Work quickly to spread the warm frosting over the first layer, stack the second on top, and then spread remaining frosting over top and sides before it sets.

Cake:
Cooking spray
2 teaspoons all-purpose flour
9 ounces all-purpose flour (about 2 cups)
¹⁄₂ teaspoon baking soda
¹⁄₂ teaspoon salt
¹⁄₂ teaspoon ground cinnamon
¹⁄₄ teaspoon ground nutmeg
Dash of ground cloves
1 cup packed brown sugar
¹⁄₂ cup butter, softened
3 large eggs
1 teaspoon vanilla extract
1 cup buttermilk
¹⁄₃ cup chopped pecans, toasted
Frosting:
¹⁄₂ cup packed brown sugar
¹⁄₄ cup heavy whipping cream
¹⁄₄ cup maple syrup
1 tablespoon butter
Dash of salt

2 cups powdered sugar
¹⁄₂ teaspoon vanilla extract
2 tablespoons chopped pecans, toasted

1. Preheat oven to 350°.
2. To prepare cake, coat 2 (8-inch) round metal cake pans with cooking spray. Line bottoms of pans with wax paper, and coat with cooking spray. Dust each pan with 1 teaspoon flour. Weigh or lightly spoon 9 ounces flour (about 2 cups) into dry measuring cups; level with a knife. Combine 9 ounces flour, baking soda, and next 4 ingredients (through cloves), stirring well with a whisk.
3. Place 1 cup brown sugar and ¹⁄₂ cup butter in a large mixing bowl; beat with a mixer at medium-high speed until light and fluffy (about 3 minutes). Add eggs, 1 at a time, beating well after each addition. Beat in 1 teaspoon vanilla. Add flour mixture and buttermilk alternately to butter mixture, beginning and ending with flour mixture and beating just until combined. Fold in ¹⁄₃ cup pecans. Divide batter evenly between prepared pans.
4. Bake at 350° for 24 minutes or until a wooden pick inserted in center comes out clean. Cool in pans 5 minutes on wire racks. Invert cake layers onto racks; cool completely. Discard wax paper.
5. To prepare frosting, place ¹⁄₂ cup brown sugar, heavy whipping cream, maple syrup, 1 tablespoon butter, and dash of salt in a heavy saucepan over medium-high heat; bring to a boil, stirring just until sugar dissolves. Cook 3 minutes, without stirring. Scrape brown sugar mixture into a bowl. Add powdered sugar; beat with a mixer at high speed 2 minutes or until slightly cooled and thick. Beat in ¹⁄₂ teaspoon vanilla. Place 1 cake layer on a plate. Spread about ³⁄₄ cup frosting evenly over 1 layer; top with second layer. Spread remaining frosting over sides and top of cake; sprinkle with 2 tablespoons pecans. Let the cake stand until frosting sets. Yield: 16 servings (serving size: 1 wedge).

CALORIES 325; FAT 11.8g (sat 5.7g, mono 3.8g, poly 1.2g); PROTEIN 3.8g; CARB 52.1g; FIBER 0.8g; CHOL 64mg; IRON 1.5mg; SODIUM 209mg; CALC 36mg

You can substitute walnuts for
pecans in this luscious cake.

KID TWEAK

Our version of this famous New England dessert boozes up the glaze with a bit of Cointreau (orange-flavored liqueur), but feel free to omit it.

Boston Cream Pie ◀

Hands-on time: 40 min. Total time: 1 hr. 20 min.
In 1855, a French chef at Boston's Parker House Hotel cooked up this variation on an older pudding-cake dish. It became the state dessert of Massachusetts.

Cake:
Cooking spray
2 teaspoons cake flour
5 ounces sifted cake flour (about 1¼ cups)
1½ teaspoons baking powder
¼ teaspoon salt
½ cup granulated sugar
¼ cup butter, softened
1 teaspoon vanilla extract
1 large egg
¾ cup 1% low-fat milk
2 large egg whites
3 tablespoons granulated sugar
Filling:
½ cup granulated sugar
3 tablespoons cornstarch
⅛ teaspoon salt
1 cup plus 2 tablespoons 1% low-fat milk
⅓ cup egg substitute
1 tablespoon butter
½ teaspoon vanilla extract
Glaze:
2 ounces dark chocolate
2 tablespoons 1% low-fat milk
⅓ cup powdered sugar
2 teaspoons Cointreau (orange-flavored liqueur)

1. Preheat oven to 350°.
2. To prepare cake, coat bottom of a 9-inch round cake pan with cooking spray. Dust with 2 teaspoons cake flour; set aside.
3. Weigh or lightly spoon 5 ounces (about 1¼ cups) flour into dry measuring cups; level with a knife. Combine flour, baking powder, and ¼ teaspoon salt in a small bowl, stirring with a whisk. Place ½ cup granulated sugar and ¼ cup butter in a large bowl, and beat with a mixer at medium speed until light and fluffy (about 5 minutes). Add 1 teaspoon vanilla and egg, beating until well blended. Add flour mixture and ¾ cup milk alternately to sugar mixture, beginning and ending with flour mixture.
4. Place egg whites in a medium bowl; beat with a mixer at high speed until foamy using clean, dry beaters. Gradually add 3 tablespoons granulated sugar, beating until stiff peaks form. Gently fold egg white mixture into batter; pour into prepared pan. Bake at 350° for 35 minutes or until a wooden pick inserted in center comes out clean. Cool in pan 10 minutes; run a knife around outside edge. Remove from pan, and cool completely on a wire rack.
5. To prepare filling, combine ½ cup granulated sugar, cornstarch, and ⅛ teaspoon salt in a medium saucepan. Gradually add 1 cup plus 2 tablespoons milk and egg substitute to pan, stirring with a whisk until well blended. Bring to a boil over medium heat, stirring constantly with a whisk until thick. Remove from heat; stir in 1 tablespoon butter and ½ teaspoon vanilla. Place pan in a large ice-filled bowl until custard cools to room temperature (about 15 minutes), stirring occasionally.
6. To prepare glaze, place chocolate and 2 tablespoons milk in a microwave-safe bowl. Microwave at HIGH 20 seconds or until chocolate melts. Add powdered sugar and liqueur, stirring with a whisk until smooth.
7. Split cake in half horizontally using a serrated knife; place bottom layer, cut side up, on a serving plate. Spread cooled filling evenly over bottom layer; top with remaining cake layer, cut side down. Spread glaze evenly over top cake layer. Yield: 10 servings (serving size: 1 piece).

CALORIES 281; **FAT** 8.7g (sat 5.2g, mono 1.9g, poly 0.4g); **PROTEIN** 5.1g; **CARB** 46.4g; **FIBER** 0.5g; **CHOL** 39mg; **IRON** 1.5mg; **SODIUM** 262mg; **CALC** 110mg

Double-Chocolate Cupcakes ◀

Hands-on time: 20 min. Total time: 38 min. These cupcakes are easy to make, and because just a few ingredients are used, it's best to purchase premium cocoa powder and dark chocolate. Since they're studded with dark chocolate chunks, dusting them with powdered sugar is enough to decorate these treats. Bake them in muffin-cup liners.

4½ ounces all-purpose flour (about 1 cup)
⅓ cup unsweetened cocoa
1 teaspoon baking soda
⅛ teaspoon salt
⅔ cup granulated sugar
¼ cup butter, softened
½ cup egg substitute
1 teaspoon vanilla
½ cup 1% low-fat buttermilk
1¼ ounces dark (70 percent cocoa) chocolate, finely chopped
2 tablespoons powdered sugar

1. Preheat oven to 350°.
2. Weigh or lightly spoon flour into a dry measuring cup; level with a knife. Combine flour, cocoa, baking soda, and salt; stir with a whisk.
3. Place granulated sugar and butter in a large bowl; beat with a mixer at medium speed until well combined (about 3 minutes). Add egg substitute and vanilla, beating well. Add flour mixture and buttermilk alternately to granulated sugar mixture, beginning and ending with flour mixture. Fold in chocolate. Spoon batter into 12 muffin cups lined with muffin cup liners. Bake at 350° for 18 minutes or until cake springs back when touched lightly in center or until a wooden pick inserted in center comes out clean. Remove from pan; cool completely on a wire rack. Sprinkle with powdered sugar just before serving. Yield: 12 servings (serving size: 1 cupcake).

CALORIES 150; **FAT** 5.2g (sat 3.2g, mono 1.2g, poly 0.2g); **PROTEIN** 3.1g; **CARB** 24g; **FIBER** 1.1g; **CHOL** 11mg; **IRON** 1mg; **SODIUM** 125mg; **CALC** 42mg

Apple Kuchen ▶

Hands-on time: 20 min. Total time: 1 hr. 5 min.

3 Fuji apples, peeled, cored, and sliced
2 tablespoons fresh lemon juice
1 cup sugar, divided
1/2 teaspoon ground cinnamon
1/2 teaspoon salt, divided
6.75 ounces all-purpose flour (about 1 1/2 cups)
1 teaspoon baking powder
1/2 cup butter, softened and divided
3 ounces cream cheese, softened
2 large eggs
1 teaspoon vanilla extract
2/3 cup nonfat buttermilk
1/2 cup chopped walnuts, toasted
Cooking spray
1/4 cup apricot preserves
2 teaspoons apple juice

1. Preheat oven to 350°.
2. Combine apples and juice; toss. Add 1/4 cup granulated sugar, ground cinnamon, and 1/4 teaspoon salt; toss to combine.
3. Weigh or lightly spoon flour into dry measuring cups; level with a knife. Combine flour, remaining 1/4 teaspoon salt, and baking powder in a bowl, stirring well. Place remaining 3/4 cup granulated sugar, 6 tablespoons butter, and cheese in a bowl; beat with a mixer at medium speed until light and fluffy. Add eggs, beating well. Stir in 1 teaspoon vanilla. Add flour mixture and buttermilk alternately to butter mixture, beginning and ending with flour mixture, beating just until combined. Stir in walnuts.
4. Scrape batter into a 13 x 9–inch metal baking pan coated with cooking spray. Arrange apples over batter. Melt remaining 2 tablespoons butter; brush over apples. Bake at 350° for 45 minutes or until set.
5. Combine preserves and juice; microwave at HIGH for 30 seconds or until melted, stirring once. Brush apricot mixture over apples; cool. Cut into 15 squares. Yield: 15 servings (serving size: 1 square).

CALORIES 251; **FAT** 11.4g (sat 5.6g, mono 2.8g, poly 2.3g); **PROTEIN** 3.9g; **CARB** 35.1g; **FIBER** 1.7g; **CHOL** 51mg; **IRON** 1mg; **SODIUM** 185mg; **CALC** 58mg

Chocolate-Orange Layer Cake ▶

Hands-on time: 40 min. Total time: 1 hr. 20 min.

Cake:

1 cup boiling water
2/3 cup unsweetened cocoa
2 ounces bittersweet chocolate, finely chopped
Cooking spray
2 teaspoons all-purpose flour
1 3/4 cups sugar
6 tablespoons butter, softened
1 teaspoon vanilla extract
3 large egg whites
1/2 cup fat-free sour cream
7.4 ounces cake flour (about 1 2/3 cups)
1 teaspoon baking powder
3/4 teaspoon baking soda
1/2 teaspoon salt

Filling:

1/3 cup orange juice
3 tablespoons sugar
1 1/2 teaspoons cornstarch
2 1/2 teaspoons unsweetened cocoa
3/4 teaspoon all-purpose flour
Dash of salt
1/4 ounce bittersweet chocolate, finely chopped
3/4 cup frozen fat-free whipped topping, thawed

Glaze:

2 tablespoons evaporated low-fat milk
1 tablespoon butter
4 ounces bittersweet chocolate, finely chopped

1. Preheat oven to 350°.
2. To prepare cake, combine 1 cup boiling water and 2/3 cup cocoa in a bowl; stir well. Add 2 ounces chocolate; stir until smooth. Cool to room temperature. Coat 2 (8-inch) round metal cake pans with cooking spray; line bottoms of pans with wax paper. Coat wax paper with cooking spray; dust each pan with 1 teaspoon flour.
3. Place 1 3/4 cups sugar, 6 tablespoons butter, and 1 teaspoon vanilla in a large mixing bowl; beat at medium speed 1 minute. Add egg whites, 1 at a time, beating well after each addition. Add sour cream; beat at medium speed 2 minutes. Weigh or lightly spoon 7.4 ounces flour (about 1 2/3 cups) into dry measuring cups; level with a knife. Combine 7.4 ounces flour, baking powder, baking soda, and 1/2 teaspoon salt in a bowl, stirring well. Add flour mixture and cocoa mixture alternately to sugar mixture, beginning and ending with flour mixture and beating just until combined.
4. Pour into prepared pans. Bake at 350° for 30 minutes or until a wooden pick inserted in center comes out clean. Cool in pans 10 minutes on wire racks. Invert layers onto racks; cool completely. Discard wax paper.
5. To prepare filling, combine juice and next 6 ingredients (through 1/4 ounce bittersweet chocolate) in a small saucepan over low heat; bring mixture to a boil, stirring frequently. Cook 1 minute, stirring constantly. Pour into a bowl. Cover and chill. Uncover; fold in whipped topping.
6. To prepare glaze, combine milk, 1 tablespoon butter, and 4 ounces chocolate in a medium microwave-safe bowl; microwave at HIGH 1 minute, stirring every 15 seconds until smooth.
7. Place 1 cake layer on a plate. Spread filling over top, leaving a 1/4-inch border. Top with remaining cake layer. Spoon warm glaze over top of cake, allowing it to drip over the edges of cake. Yield: 16 servings (serving size: 1 wedge).

CALORIES 280; **FAT** 10.4g (sat 5.7g, mono 1.3g, poly 0.3g); **PROTEIN** 4.2g; **CARB** 46g; **FIBER** 1.9g; **CHOL** 14mg; **IRON** 1.5mg; **SODIUM** 229mg; **CALC** 38mg

A majestic homemade layer cake puts the exclamation point on your dinner table.

Walnut Cupcakes with Maple Frosting ◄

Hands-on time: 25 min. Total time: 45 min.

Cupcakes:
½ cup granulated sugar
½ cup packed brown sugar
6 tablespoons butter, softened
3 large eggs
1 teaspoon vanilla extract
8 ounces cake flour (about 2 cups)
½ teaspoon baking soda
¼ teaspoon salt
¼ teaspoon ground cinnamon
½ cup buttermilk
⅓ cup plus 2 tablespoons walnuts, toasted, chopped, and divided

Frosting:
½ teaspoon cream of tartar
3 large egg whites
¾ cup maple sugar or granulated sugar
¼ cup water
Dash of salt

1. Preheat oven to 350°.
2. Combine first 3 ingredients in a medium bowl; beat with a mixer at medium speed. Add eggs, 1 at a time, beating well after each addition. Stir in vanilla. Increase speed to high; beat for 1 minute.
3. Weigh flour. Combine flour and next 3 ingredients (through cinnamon), stirring well. Add flour mixture and buttermilk alternately to sugar mixture, beginning and ending with flour mixture, beating until just combined. Stir in ⅓ cup walnuts.
4. Place 12 muffin cup liners in muffin cups; divide batter evenly among cups. Bake at 350° for 19 minutes or until a wooden pick inserted in center comes out with moist crumbs clinging. (Cupcakes will look slightly pale.) Cool in pan 5 minutes. Remove from pan; cool on wire rack.
5. Place cream of tartar and egg whites in a large bowl; beat with a mixer at high speed until soft peaks form. Combine maple sugar, ¼ cup water, and dash of salt in a small saucepan; bring to a boil. Cook, without stirring, until candy thermometer registers 238°. Gradually pour hot sugar syrup into egg white mixture,

beating until stiff peaks form. Spread about 3 rounded tablespoonfuls frosting over each cupcake. Sprinkle with remaining 2 tablespoons nuts. Yield: 12 servings (serving size: 1 cupcake).

CALORIES 291; **FAT** 10.4g (sat 4.5g, mono 2.4g, poly 2.6g); **PROTEIN** 5.4g; **CARB** 44.7g; **FIBER** 0.7g; **CHOL** 69mg; **IRON** 2.4mg; **SODIUM** 203mg; **CALC** 33mg

Caramel Layer Cake ▲

Hands-on time: 35 min. Total time: 1 hr. Work quickly to spread the cooked frosting on the cake layers before it begins to set.

Cake:
Cooking spray
1 tablespoon cake flour
1 cup packed light brown sugar
7 tablespoons butter, softened
½ cup egg substitute
8 ounces cake flour (about 2 cups)
1 teaspoon baking powder
½ teaspoon baking soda
¼ teaspoon salt
1 cup fat-free milk

Frosting:
½ cup packed dark brown sugar
3 tablespoons butter
1 teaspoon vanilla extract
⅛ teaspoon salt
1 (14-ounce) can sweetened condensed milk

1. Preheat oven to 350°.
2. To prepare cake, coat 2 (8-inch) round cake pans with cooking spray; line bottoms of pans with wax paper.

Lightly coat wax paper with cooking spray; dust with 1 tablespoon flour.
3. Place 1 cup light brown sugar and 7 tablespoons butter in a large mixing bowl; beat with a mixer at medium speed 3 minutes or until well blended. Add egg substitute to sugar mixture; beat well. Weigh or lightly spoon 2 cups cake flour into dry measuring cups; level with a knife. Combine cake flour, baking powder, baking soda, and ¼ teaspoon salt, stirring well with a whisk. Add flour mixture to sugar mixture alternately with 1 cup fat-free milk, beginning and ending with the flour mixture.
4. Spoon batter into prepared pans. Sharply tap pans once on counter to remove air bubbles. Bake at 350° for 25 minutes or until a wooden pick inserted in center comes out clean. Cool in pans 10 minutes on wire racks. Invert cake layers onto racks; remove pans. Cool layers completely on wire racks. Discard wax paper.
5. To prepare frosting, combine ½ cup dark brown sugar and remaining ingredients in a medium heavy saucepan over medium heat; bring to a boil. Cook 2 minutes or until mixture is thick, stirring constantly.
6. Place 1 cake layer on a plate; spread with ⅓ cup frosting. Top with remaining cake layer. Spread remaining frosting over top and sides of cake. Yield: 16 servings (serving size: 1 slice).

CALORIES 298; **FAT** 9.7g (sat 6g, mono 2.5g, poly 0.5g); **PROTEIN** 5g; **CARB** 48.5g; **FIBER** 0.3g; **CHOL** 28mg; **IRON** 1.9mg; **SODIUM** 238mg; **CALC** 136mg

{ fyi }

Made-from-scratch cakes have great make-ahead potential. You can bake layers up to a month ahead and freeze, and most fillings and frostings can be made ahead of time, as well. All you need to do is thaw and assemble the day before.

The information in the following charts is provided to help cooks outside the United States successfully use the recipes in this book. All equivalents are approximate.

COOKING/ OVEN TEMPERATURES

	FAHRENHEIT	CELSIUS	GAS MARK
FREEZE WATER	32°F	0°C	
ROOM TEMPERATURE	68°F	20°C	
BOIL WATER	212°F	100°C	
BAKE	325°F	160°C	3
	350°F	180°C	4
	375°F	190°C	5
	400°F	200°C	6
	425°F	220°C	7
	450°F	230°C	8
BROIL			Grill

LIQUID INGREDIENTS BY VOLUME

¼ tsp					=	1 ml
½ tsp					=	2 ml
1 tsp					=	5 ml
3 tsp	= 1 tbl			= ½ fl oz	=	15 ml
	2 tbls	= ⅛ cup	= 1 fl oz		=	30 ml
	4 tbls	= ¼ cup	= 2 fl oz		=	60 ml
	5⅓ tbls	= ⅓ cup	= 3 fl oz		=	80 ml
	8 tbls	= ½ cup	= 4 fl oz		=	120 ml
	10⅔ tbls	= ⅔ cup	= 5 fl oz		=	160 ml
	12 tbls	= ¾ cup	= 6 fl oz		=	180 ml
	16 tbls	= 1 cup	= 8 fl oz		=	240 ml
	1 pt	= 2 cups	= 16 fl oz		=	480 ml
	1 qt	= 4 cups	= 32 fl oz		=	960 ml
			33 fl oz	= 1,000 ml	=	1 l

EQUIVALENTS FOR DIFFERENT TYPES OF INGREDIENTS

STANDARD CUP	FINE POWDER (ex. flour)	GRAIN (ex. rice)	GRANULAR (ex. sugar)	LIQUID SOLIDS (ex. butter)	LIQUID (ex. milk)
1	140g	150g	190g	200g	240 ml
¾	105g	113g	143g	150g	180 ml
⅔	93g	100g	125g	133g	160 ml
½	70g	75g	95g	100g	120 ml
⅓	47g	50g	63g	67g	80 ml
¼	35g	38g	48g	50g	60 ml
⅛	18g	19g	24g	25g	30 ml

DRY INGREDIENTS BY WEIGHT

To convert ounces to grams, multiply the number of ounces by 30.

1 oz	=	¹⁄₁₆ lb	=	30g
4 oz	=	¼ lb	=	120g
8 oz	=	½ lb	=	240g
12 oz	=	¾ lb	=	360g
16 oz	=	1 lb	=	480g

LENGTH

To convert inches to centimeters, multiply the number of inches by 2.5.

1 in	=			2.5 cm		
6 in	=	½ ft	=	15 cm		
12 in	=	1 ft	=	30 cm		
36 in	=	3 ft	= 1 yd	= 90 cm		
40 in	=			100 cm	=	1 m

HOW TO USE IT AND WHY

Glance at the end of any *Cooking Light* recipe, and you'll see how committed we to helping you make the best of today's light cooking. With four chefs, two registered dietitians, three home economists, and a computer system that analyzes every ingredient we use, *Cooking Light* gives you authoritative dietary detail that you won't find in any other epicurean magazine.

We go to great lengths to show you how our recipes fit into your healthful eating plan. If you're trying to lose weight, the calorie and fat figures probably will help most. But if you're keeping a close eye on the sodium, cholesterol, and saturated fat in your diet, we provide those numbers, too. And because many women don't get enough iron or calcium, we can help you there. Finally, there's a fiber analysis to help you make sure that you get enough roughage.

WHAT IT MEANS AND HOW WE GET THERE

Besides the calories, protein, fat, fiber, iron, and sodium we list at the end of each recipe, there are a few things we abbreviate for space.

- **sat** saturated fat
- **carb** carbohydrates
- **g** gram

- **mono** monounsaturated fat
- **chol** cholesterol
- **mg** milligram

- **poly** polyunsaturated fat
- **calc** calcium

We get numbers for those categories based on a few assumptions:

- When we give a range for an ingredient (3 to 3½ cups flour, for instance), we calculate the lesser amount.
- Some alcohol calories evaporate during heating; we reflect that.
- Only the amount of marinade absorbed by the food is calculated.

YOUR DAILY NUTRITION GUIDE

	WOMEN ages 25 to 50	WOMEN over 50	MEN over 24
CALORIES	2,000	2,000 or less	2,700
PROTEIN	50g	50g or less	63g
FAT	65g or less	65g or less	88g or less
SATURATED FAT	20g or less	20g or less	27g or less
CARBOHYDRATES	304g	304g	410g
FIBER	25g to 35g	25g to 35g	25g to 35g
CHOLESTEROL	300mg or less	300mg or less	300mg or less
IRON	18mg	8mg	8mg
SODIUM	2,300mg or less	1,500mg or less	2,300mg or less
CALCIUM	1,000mg	1,200mg	1,000mg

Calorie requirements vary according to your gender, size, weight, and level of physical activity. This chart is a good general guide for healthy adults. Additional nutrients are needed during some stages of life. For example, children's calorie and protein needs are based on their height and vary greatly as they grow. Teenagers require less protein but need more calcium and slightly more iron than adults. Pregnant or breast-feeding women need more protein, calories, and calcium. The need for iron increases during pregnancy but returns to normal after delivery.

THE NUTRITIONAL VALUES USED IN OUR CALCULATIONS EITHER COME FROM A COMPUTER PROGRAM PRODUCED BY COMPUTRITION INC., THE FOOD PROCESSOR, VERSION 7.5 (ESHA RESEARCH), OR ARE PROVIDED BY FOOD MANUFACTURERS.

BROWNIES AND BARS

CAKES AND CUPCAKES

COOKIES

MUFFINS AND SCONES

PANCAKES, ETC.

Pecan Spice Cake with Maple Frosting, page 86

PIES, PASTRIES, AND CHEESECAKES

QUICK BREAD LOAVES

YEAST BREADS

YEAST ROLLS